Writer's Book Shelf

I0201990

Inside the Cover

Fonts, Formatting & Final Touches

Carol Peterson

Honor Bound Books

Honor Bound Books

Cover background, certain images created or adjusted using Photoshop Elements used with license from Adobe. Interior fonts used with permission from Microsoft. Font styles used include Cambria, Calibri, Arial, Georgia, Sogona, Viner Hand, Bradley Hand, Brush Script MT, Chiller, Tahoma, Verdana, Wingdings, and Wingdings 2. Some graphics from Pixabay.com used with permission.

ISBN-13: 978-1-951587-04-8

Dedication

This book is dedicated to writers endeavoring to independently publish their books, with the hope that it will encourage them to follow and customize publishing industry standards so their work will be recognized as professionally presented to their readers.

Of making many books there is no end,

and much study wearies the body

(Ecclesiastes 12:12 NIV).

Table of Contents

Acknowledgment

My thanks to my writing colleague, Mary Vine for her editing of this book. Mary writes light Christian romance novels that take place in Oregon and Idaho. You can find her online at AuthorMaryVine.blogspot.com.

My thanks also to my writing colleague, JoEllen Claypool for her encouragement about this book and for her kind words in the Foreword. You can find her online at JoEllenClaypool.com.

Thank you also to my husband, Jim who counseled me on wording of steps in implementing tools on Microsoft Word so readers will be encouraged even if their screen is not identical to the screen shots in this book.

Foreword

As a writer, when a book idea pops into our head, eagerness can overcome good sense. We are only focused on becoming a published author or getting another book out there for the world to see. However, there is so much more to it than throwing words on paper to cover the information you are trying to convey.

As a reader, a person wants to know that they can trust the author. If you want to have credibility with your reader, you will have to put the effort into the layout of each page inside your book's cover. Once your reader has been drawn to your cover and has been hooked by the information on the back of the book, now is the time to impress them with the rest!

As an editor, the visual aspect of your book's interior will further prove the professionalism of your trade. Your goal is to be thorough from the title page and copyright page all the way through to the bibliography and index pages and everything in between. The valuable information provided in Carol Peterson's book, *Inside the Cover*, will help you do just that. It will explain and guide you through each step of the process and provide you with the opportunity to turn out a quality product.

Enjoy your writing journey!

JoEllen Claypool
Author/Editor

Preface

When I began my writing journey as a children's writer, I was fascinated by the way words and pictures worked together to weave something beautiful for children. Not only did the illustrations in picture books complement the stories, they had the power to influence pacing and theme or even tell an opposite story visually.

All books in fact contain important visual elements. Except for audio books, we hold physical books in our hands and look at them. Even e-Books we read visually, even if on a screen. The words and other visual elements are experienced through our sense of sight.

As independently published authors, we also can use visual elements to make our books more wonderful for our readers. Your book can be more than a wonderful story or more than a compilation of thoughts or advice. It can be a total reading experience, using specific formatting, layout, and embellishments that enrich the reading adventure.

Introduction

Maybe you have spent seven years writing and editing your book. Or maybe you have spent a lifetime doing so. The story or information organization is wonderful. The writing is beautiful. Your editor has made sure each period and comma are properly placed.

Your book is perfect.

But it could be made even better by the physical layout of the book. That's what this book is about.

Information in *Inside the Cover* is organized from the larger physical aspects—book trim size and formatting of your manuscript—to more specialized elements—selecting fonts and adding chapter icons, décor, or detail. Each chapter provides a summary statement and prompts to implement items discussed in that chapter. Where needed, specific steps and screen shots are included.

All instructions in the book are for the specific steps I took to create this book. That means you hold a physical example of what the end result will look like if you follow those steps.

While this is a how-to book on interior formatting, it is also an idea book. Not every concept will be perfect for the book you are working on right now. But some will be. Others might be perfect for your next book. Or your 42nd book.

While reading this book, focus on how your own book is a physical product that contains not just entertaining stories or illuminating concepts. Your book is also a visual experience for your reader. Why not make your book even more wonderful for your readers by adding visual elements to enhance your reader's experience and make them love your book and you as an author who has created something with them in mind?

One reminder while reading this book: I have provided step-by-step instructions and screen shots of Microsoft Word on how I set up parts of this book. Please remember that the version of Microsoft Word I have may not be exactly the same version you are using. Additionally, your version may have been customized or reconfigured in a slightly different way from mine. Therefore the steps and screen shots may be slightly different from what appears on your own computer screen.

This book is not a book on how to use Microsoft Word. It is intended to give guidance on what to look for in your own word processing program, by giving you steps and visual cues for where tools might be located or what terms to look for. If the steps or screen shots in this book differ from what your computer screen shows, I encourage you to search online, using the terms presented in this book. New online tutorials show up continuously and you may find exactly what you need to answer your individual questions for how to use your own word processing software.

The main purpose for the steps and screen shots in this book is to inform you of what things you might do to format your manuscript visually by sharing what I have done specifically so that you have both a visual example of the finished product and the information of how I accomplished that.

Most writers struggle with the technology aspect of writing and publishing. Hopefully the terms and thoughts presented in this book will encourage you. After all, if I can ultimately learn something new about the technology of publishing—a person who regularly can't figure out how to answer her cell phone—so can you.

Stay encouraged!

Inside the Cover

Chapter 1

Words Are not Enough

Imagine your book sitting on the shelf at the local bookstore. Let's enjoy that image for a minute. Ahhh, there it is. Top shelf. Spine out. Proudly displaying its title.

That title is so creative. That title urges the buyer to slide the book out from the shelf and turn it over to see the front cover.

The front cover that is so striking. That cover entices the buyer to open the book to see what's inside.

The buyer opens the book and flips through the pages. She reads the Foreword. Stops at the Table of Contents. Scans the chapters.

One. Two. Three. And that's it. She'll either slip the book back on the shelf or take it home.

Three chances to help your reader decide to buy your book. In less than a minute.

The first chance you have is the title. Does it entice? Does it provide enough information for the reader to want more? Is it clever or mysterious or pithy?

Words are not Enough

The second chance you have is the cover. Does it convey the genre of your book? The emotional feel of the book? Does it hint at what is inside? Does the back copy explain enough to intrigue the buyer?

The third chance is physical layout of your book. When a buyer opens your book, does the interior look professional or does it scream newbie, self-published, or haphazard?

Even before a person reads a single word of your wonderful book, the interior of the book—the layout, the fonts used, the way the chapters are presented visually—all can either further encourage the person to buy your book or put it back on the shelf.

The interior layout of your book is your third chance to impress that buyer and turn him into your reader. It could be your last chance.

No matter how brilliant your story, no matter how important your topic, no matter what wonderful words you have written, if you have not visually presented your manuscript in a way that augments your book, you may be losing readers.

Furthermore, a book is not just a compilation of words. It is not just a presentation of thoughts or story. A book is a product that people hold in their hands—even if it is inside an electronic device.

A book is not just an intellectual or emotional experience. Unless it is turned into an audio book, it is also a visual experience. How the manuscript is presented visually is part of the experience for the reader as a whole. Why not make that experience better, more effective, and more powerful for your reader?

That's what this book is about. This book is about knowing what decisions to make about your book's physical layout and why they are important. It is also about making decisions on purpose to achieve those effects.

Words are not Enough

This book will assume you are a writer who is fairly new at book production. There will be parts of this book that therefore simplify the technical process of formatting your manuscript using Microsoft Word. I have provided screen shots and step-by-step instructions for you to follow more easily.

If you are not new to independent publishing, however, stay tuned. This book is chock full of ideas you may have never considered for how to give your book interior pow!

This book also assumes that you will be independent publishing through Amazon publishing services, specifically via (Kindle Direct Publishing) for both print on demand and Kindle eBooks. Therefore, I have provided technical information relating to what Amazon requires.

For more concrete and practical help, I explain how I achieved the format and layout of this particular book. That way you can see the steps I took to achieve the results you hold in your hands.

At the end of each chapter are key summary points and prompts to help you make decisions for the layout of your book project. At the end of the book, I have also provided appendices to help you plan and keep track of your book projects.

I hope this book will be an encouragement to you as you expand the scope of your book's interior to present it as a cohesive, wonderful product for your reader to hold in her hands and love.

Do you have a book you are ready to format for publication? Do you have thoughts on what you want the interior to look like?

Checklist

☐ Book title I'm working on: _____

☐ My book's genre: _____

Chapter 2

Size Matters: Industry Standards

A book's size has a lot to do with its purpose. A coffee table book of full-page photographs, for example, is typically 8 x 11 or larger. Part of the experience for the reader of coffee table books is holding it in his hands, feeling the smoothness of the full-page glossy photographs as he turns the pages. The weight of the book and the pages themselves gives the reader a physical sense of luxury and peace. Part of a coffee table book's value comes from the physical way the book has been put together.

Similarly, a children's picture book is usually square, sized at 7.5 x 7.5, 8.5 x 8.5 or 9 x 9. The interior colorful artwork is printed on white paper, so the colors remain true. Some artwork extends to the very edge of the pages. The glossy cover attracts the child's attention and makes her want to pick up the book and see what fun is inside. Part of a picture book's value comes from the physical way the book has been put together.

You will therefore want to consider many aspects of the book's size and layout for your particular book. In this chapter, we will look specifically at size.

Why Follow Industry Size Standards?

While independent publishing allows for the author to make his own decisions, following publishing industry standards gives professional credibility to the author. It also gives a reader a sense of familiarity, picking up a book in the size she expects it to be—whether or not she knows what publishing industry standards are.

This sense of familiarity comes from the fact that genres are sized specifically for that genre within publishing industry standards. When a reader of that genre picks up a book properly sized for that genre, she will recognize it as "legitimate" for that genre. The author will already have gained a degree of the reader's respect for having followed the rules.

While you want your book to stand out, you want it to stand out in a manner that is professional. Following industry standards is a way you can do so. Conforming to industry and genre standards may help legitimize your book in the eyes of your readers. Not conforming may do the opposite.

Industry Size Standards by Genre

Industry standards are linked closely to genre. Here is a listing of industry standard sizes to help you make a selection for your book. The specific term for book size, is *trim size.* Amazon and other publishing entities will use that term. You should become aware of it also.

Fiction (Novel)

- 4.25" x 6.87" (mass market) This is the typical paperback book size (trim size). It is not currently available on Amazon publishing. Additionally, if you decide to publish independently elsewhere, you should keep in mind that a smaller sized book will need to also have a smaller sized font, which may influence your reader's choice to purchase it or one which is easier to read.

- 5" x 8" (trade)

- 5.25" x 8" (trade)

- 5.5" x 8.5" (trade/digest)

- 6" by 9" This is the most popular size on Amazon publishing. It also allows you to increase the size of the font while maintaining a reasonable page length—popular with readers who may struggle with eyesight or a need for more white space on the page.

- 5" x 8" (Novella)

Children's Books

- 7.5" x 7.5" (or 8" x 8" or 8.5" x 8.5" or 9" x 9") Picture books

- 10" x 8"

- 6" x 9" early readers; middle grade novels

Nonfiction

- 5.5" x 8.5" (trade)

- 6" x 9"

- 7" by 10"

Memoir

- 5.25" x 8"

- 5.5" x 8.5"

Textbooks

- 6" x 9"

- 7" x 10"

- 8.5" x 11"

Photography (including "Coffee Table Books") any size up to 8.5" x 11.

Now that you have a sense of what size readers expect for your book, it is time to make some decisions and create the technical files to properly format your files.

Before beginning the publication process, you first need to determine the best trim size for your particular book.

Checklist

☐ My book genre: _____

☐ The best trim size for my book: _____

Chapter 3

Sizing Your Manuscript

Once you have determined the best trim size for your book, the first thing to do is set up your Microsoft Word file so your manuscript will be sized appropriately.

Terms in This Chapter

Trim size of your book: the paper size in Microsoft Office

Margins: the white space between the manuscript (text) and the outside edges

Gutter: what it is; what it should be set at (larger for longer books over 150 pages)

Mirror pages: this setting will assure that the margins on both the left page and the right page are identical.

First page different: this allows you to not include a page number or header on the odd-numbered beginning pages of new chapters.

The **Ribbon** in Microsoft Word refers to the horizontal section of your Microsoft screen, above the white space where you type. The Ribbon contains clickable instructions to help you customize your manuscript. At the top of the ribbon are tabs. When you click on those tabs, the contents of the Ribbon change.

For purposes of illustration, I will show you how to set up a book layout in Microsoft Word. I will specifically share with you the mechanics I used to set up *this book* manuscript. That way, when you see what settings I have used, you will also have an example of what they look like in the final, printed book.

I suggest then, that you go through the steps and set up a document, using the settings you regularly plan to use for your own book publishing. Leave that document blank and label it appropriately. For example:

6 x 9 BOOK TEMPLATE

Whenever you begin a new book, open that file, rename it with your book title and you're all set to go. Plus, by renaming it, you will still have your book template ready for the next book. And the next.

Steps to Manuscript Formatting

Remember: your version of Microsoft Word may be a different version from the one I have used or your screen may have been customized or reconfigured. If these steps and screen shots are different from what appears on your screen, please stay calm and search online, using the terms in this section to find instructions or tutorials that work for your particular software. You can do this!

Open a new Microsoft Word file. Go to the **Layout** tab on the Ribbon.

Sizing Your Manuscript

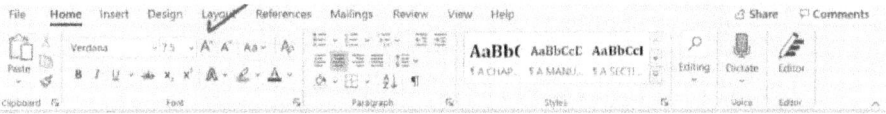

Size: First we will set the size of the manuscript based on the book's trim size.

Go to **Layout**→Size

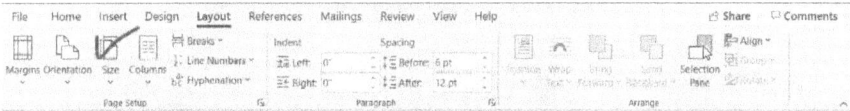

Click on down arrow to open dialogue box

Click on more paper sizes→**Custom Size**

Type size (e.g., 6" x 9" like this book)

Click **Whole Document** at bottom of the open tab.

Click OK.

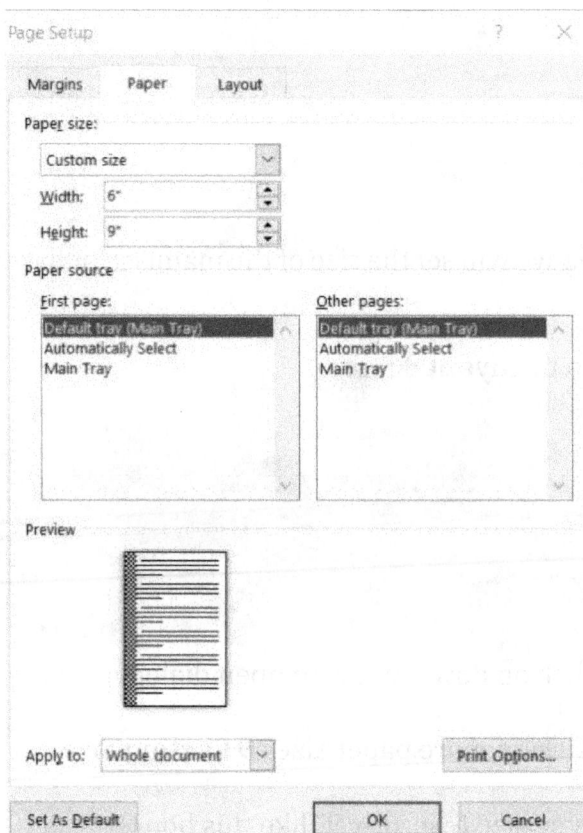

You have now set the manuscript size for the book's trim size you have selected.

Margins: Now set your margins for your book. Go back to the **Layout** tab on the Ribbon . Then select **Margins**. From the dialogue box, select **Custom Margins**.

Standard margins for a book are .5" on the top, bottom, and outside margins. Leave the inside margin at .0 inch. Instead of the inside margin, set a gutter. The gutter refers to the center section of the book.

The gutter size is dependent on the number of pages you will have in your book. This is because, the thicker your book, the harder it is physically to open the book at the center. Words therefore are in danger of being lost inside the crease of the book. As a result, for longer books, the gutter margin must be larger.

Here is the standard chart to use to set your gutter. When determining your gutter size, make sure to include the pages you will have in both your front and back matter. See Chapters 15 and 15 for what you might include in your book.

24-150 pages gutter .375"
151 – 400 pages gutter .75"
401 to 600 pages gutter .875"
More than 600 pages gutter 1.0"

For our example, let's assume a book with a page length of more than 150 pages, but less than 400.

Also make sure to select **Portrait** orientation; multiple pages: **Mirror Margins** and apply to: **Whole Document**. Then click OK.

Here is what the **Margins** dialogue box should look like:

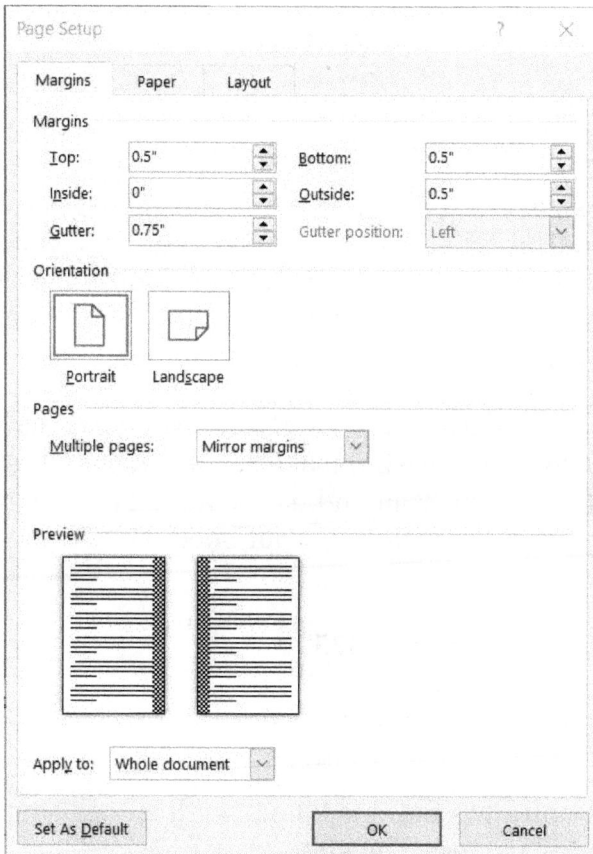

The above should now complete your set up for your book manuscript, not including how you want your text paragraphs formatted.

Full Bleed: There is one additional step you need to take if you want full bleed for your manuscript. Full bleed refers to the formatting that allows illustrations, photographs or other graphics to be printed to the very edge of the page. This is typical for some picture books or for books with full page or full spread (the two pages of an open book) photographs. To format your layout for full bleed, you must add .125" to the book's width and .25" to its height. That means for our example, the manuscript size will be 6.125" x 9.25."

When setting up for full bleed, you must also readjust the margins. Leave the gutter set for the appropriate number of pages. But then set the other three outside margins to 0. When you try to close the dialogue box, Microsoft Word may ding and tell you "some margins are outside the printable area. Fix/Ignore."

The point with full bleed is that you want the edges to extend beyond the printable area. So, click IGNORE and close the dialogue box. The document is properly formatted for full bleed for Amazon.

White Space: Adequate white space (where text does not appear) makes it easy on the reader's eyes. Some authors like to make very narrow margins or use very small font size in order to lower the cost of printing and thus maintain higher royalties.

As authors, of course we want to make money. Our first and utmost consideration, however, should always be our readers. If a little extra white space keeps our readers' eyes from straining and thus keeps them reading, we should give them that white space on the page.

It is time to decide on your book's trim size, estimate your book page length and gutter needed, and determine the margins for your manuscript.

Checklist

- ☐ My book's trim size is: _____

- ☐ I estimate my number of pages will be (including front matter and back matter): _____

- ☐ Therefore, my gutter needs to be: _____

- ☐ My Margins will be:
  Top: _____
  Bottom: _____
  Outside: _____

Chapter 4

What's Your Style?

It can be jarring to your readers if your manuscript suddenly switches fonts. Or if, out of the blue, your tidy justified margins turn ragged and then back again. Any time a reader must focus on something other than what you have written, it takes away from their reading experience and reduces the effectiveness of your writing.

We don't want that.

Therefore, it is important to keep our formatting consistent throughout our book. We can do that easiest by using the powerful tool available to us in Microsoft Word: **Styles**.

I had written a dozen books and had used Microsoft Word in its various iterations for over 20 years before I ever heard about Styles. I have scratched the surface of what Styles can do, but I do know for sure that I will never go back to trying to create a book without using Styles. It is powerful, easy to use, and flat-out helps you create a professional product with little effort.

It will also simplify editing. Using Styles, you do not have to worry about making sure indents, margins, and titles are consistent throughout. It's a fabulous tool. Don't be afraid of it.

To help those of you like me who are firmly ensconced in the "untechie" realm, I'll simplify the process for you and define some of the terms you might encounter or need to know as you wind your way through Microsoft Word.

Remember: your version of Microsoft Word may be a different version from mine, or your screen may have been customized or reconfigured. If these steps and screen shots are different from what appears on your screen, please stay calm and search online, using the terms in this section to find instructions or tutorials that work for your particular software. You can do this!

Here we go.

◆◆◆

While Word has some good pre-set Styles, it can be helpful for you to specifically and consciously create your own Styles, so you know what they are and don't click on an incorrect Style by mistake.

To set up your Styles, first make sure you are on the **Home** screen tab on the Ribbon. There, at the bottom of the Ribbon, in small letters is the word Styles. Next to the word Styles, is a small square and downward-and-to-the-right arrow. Click on that square to open the Styles sidebar.

What's Your Style?

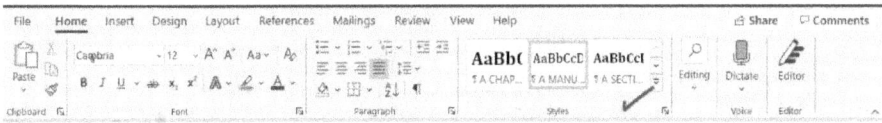

The Styles sidebar should open to the right of your Word document screen, similar to a sidebar on a website or print magazine.

The Styles sidebar is similar to the Ribbon at the top of your Word document but limited just to using the Microsoft Styles you will use to format your document.

Here is where we will set up our own Styles.

What's Your Style?

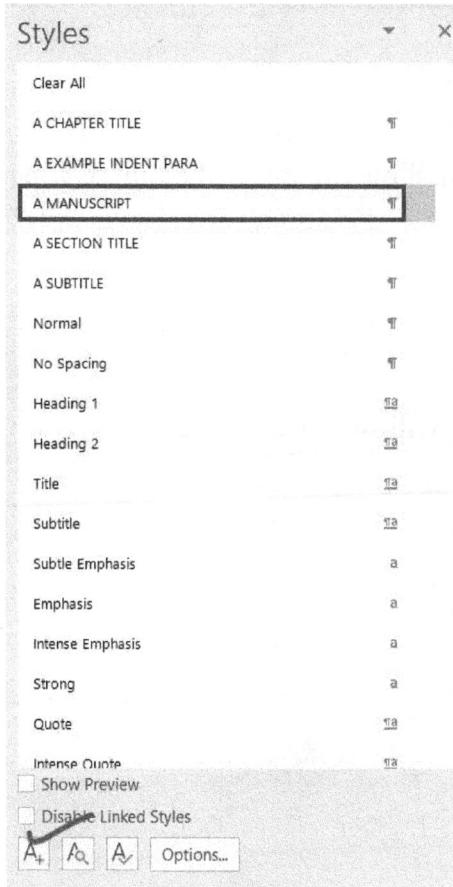

At the very bottom of the Styles sidebar is a capital A followed by +. Click on that A+ box to create a new Style.

First name the Style. I suggest you name the Style with the capital letter A→space→simple title.

By naming the Style first with an A, that personalized style will show up at the top of the Styles list where you can find it easily. I also suggest you name each of your Styles in all caps to be able to easily see which ones you have created, since the pre-set Styles are all in upper/lower case names.

Setting up a Manuscript Body Style

For this example we have decided we do not want to indent the first line of paragraphs and will have one extra line between paragraphs. We want our font to be Cambria 12 point. We also want full justified margins for our manuscript. Those are the same settings I have used for this book.

Open **Styles**→click on **A+ Create new style**

Name it: A MANUSCRIPT

Leave **Style type**, **Based on**, and **Style for Paragraph** as defaulted.

Select the font style and size and both justified. For this book, I have used Cambria 12 point. Leave the font color as automatic. Do not select bold, italic, or underlined.

Go then to the **Format** tab located at the bottom left of that screen. Click the down arrow and open **Paragraph**. There do not select any indentation but do add 6 pt spacing above and 12 pt below line. Do *not* check the box "**Don't add space between paragraphs of same style**." Leave that box unchecked because we *do want* that extra line space between paragraphs. Also, leave the line spacing at single.

Paragraph ? ×

Indents and Spacing   Line and Page Breaks

General

Alignment: Justified

Outline level: Body Text   ☐ Collapsed by default

Indentation

Left: 0"

Right: 0"   Special: (none)   By:

☐ Mirror indents

Spacing

Before: 6 pt

After: 12 pt   Line spacing: Single   At:

☐ Don't add space between paragraphs of the same style

Preview

Previous Paragraph Previous Paragraph Previous Paragraph Previous Paragraph Previous Paragraph Previous Paragraph Previous Paragraph Previous Paragraph Previous Paragraph
Sample Text Sample Text
Following Paragraph Following Paragraph Following Paragraph Following Paragraph Following Paragraph Following Paragraph Following Paragraph Following Paragraph

Tabs...   Set As Default   OK   Cancel

Then Click OK and you have created a style for the body of your manuscript.

Alternate Formatting for Indented Paragraphs:

If you want to have the first line indented with no spaces between paragraphs—like this paragraph and the next two in this book, here is how to do that.

What's Your Style?

On the **Paragraph** tab on the **Styles** dialogue box, instead of doing the above steps, do this:

Select the **Special→First Line**. To the right, select .5". That will indent the first line only of each paragraph. DO NOT click on the left or right **Indentation** as that will indent the entire paragraph.

Paragraph		?	✕

Indents and Spacing   Line and Page Breaks

General

Alignment:	Justified ⌄	
Outline level:	Body Text ⌄	☐ Collapsed by default

Indentation

Left:	0" ⬍	Special:	By:
Right:	0" ⬍	First line ⌄	0.5" ⬍

☐ Mirror indents

Spacing

Before:	0 pt ⬍	Line spacing:	At:
After:	0 pt ⬍	Single ⌄	⬍

☑ Don't add space between paragraphs of the same style

Preview

Previous Paragraph Previous Paragraph Previous Paragraph Previous Paragraph Previous Paragraph Previous Paragraph Previous Paragraph Previous Paragraph Previous Paragraph Previous Paragraph
Sample Text Sample Text Sample Text Sample Text Sample Text Sample Text Sample Text Sample Text Sample Text Sample Text Sample Text Sample Text Sample Text Sample Text Sample Text Sample Text Sample Text Sample Text Sample Text Sample Text
Following Paragraph Following Paragraph Following Paragraph Following Paragraph Following Paragraph Following Paragraph Following Paragraph Following Paragraph Following Paragraph Following Paragraph Following Paragraph Following Paragraph Following Paragraph Following Paragraph Following Paragraph Following Paragraph

Tabs...	Set As Default	OK	Cancel

Make sure to check the **Don't add space between paragraphs of the same style.**

Other Styles

Follow the same steps to create the chapter titles and subtitles you plan to use. You may want the chapter titles in a larger size font and bold and centered on the page. You may also want the chapter titles to set lower on the page. To do so, adjust the spacing **Before** and **After** when creating the **Style.** When you select it during typing, it will automatically take your cursor to the proper place for the title.

My preference for chapter titles as used in this book is to use Cambria bold 16 pt font size. Create the spacing before and after by clicking on the **Format→Paragraph→Indent and Spacing→ Spacing** for the **Style** you create. Enter 144 before and 18 after and single spacing. The two screens look like this:

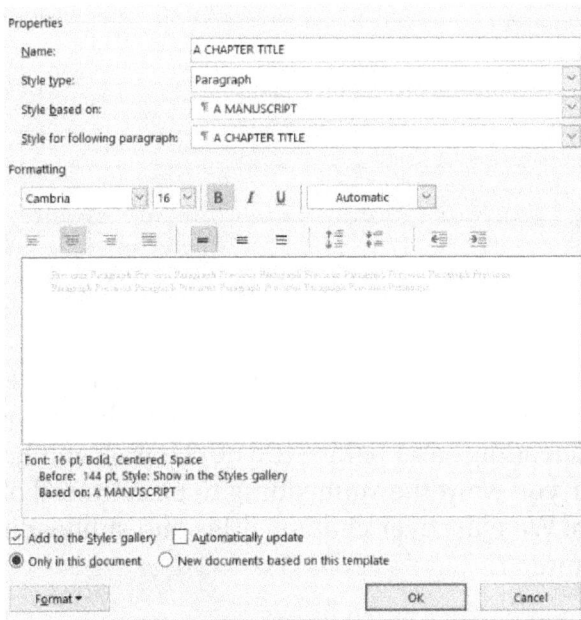

and

You may decide to make subheadings in a smaller sized font than the chapter title and you will want less space before and possibly after the subheadings and before the next paragraph begins. Select also whether you want the subheading to be centered or at the left-hand margin. We will cover chapter titles and subheadings in more detail in Chapter 7.

You may want to set up other specific **Styles** for your individual manuscript. I set up a **Style** for Scripture when I quote Bible verses within my manuscripts. I set that **Style** for indented .5" from both left and right margins. There is no additional first line indent. All is in the same font style and size but set in italics. Like this:

> *writing books is endless, and much study wears you out* (Ecclesiastes 12:12).

I also routinely create a **Style** for places in books where I ask readers questions or pose a challenge. My **Style** then often provides space for them to write their answer in the book.

Think through your manuscript and see what **Styles** you might create to help keep your book layout consistent and simplify the formatting and editing process.

If you later decide you want to change the font or spacing of a particular **Style**, you can either start over and create a new one or modify the current one. To modify a **Style**, go to the **Styles** sidebar and right click on the specific **Style** you want to modify. Left click on the option **Modify**. It will open the dialogue box as if you were creating a new **Style**, but the existing choices will be displayed. Simply change whichever parts of the **Style** you wish to change and then click OK.

Styles is a powerful tool. I personally only use a portion of what it is capable of doing. I have tried to keep things simple for you, by sharing what I use. Please feel free to expand your knowledge of this tool to help you make your books fabulous!

It's time to decide on the formatting for the Styles
you will use in your manuscript layout.

Checklist

☐ I want/do not want indented paragraphs _____

☐ Font type and size I will use _____ (see Chapter 9 for more on fonts)

☐ I need the following Styles in addition to chapter titles and paragraphs:

_____

_____

_____

Chapter 5

Legal Mumbo Jumbo

Another thing to prepare in the initial stages of your book's production is the legal information you will need for publication. Those items include your ISBN, your copyright, and your book's barcode. Here's some of what you need to know.

ISBN

You must have an ISB number for your printed book to be sold commercially. An **ISBN** refers to the book's international standard book number. It is a ten or 13-digit number assigned to every book before publication. It records details such as the book's language, location of publication, and publisher.

These ISBNs in the United States are regulated, monitored, and sold through Bowker Identifier Services. You may purchase an individual ISBN from them or may purchase them in bulk at a lower per ISBN cost. The ISBNs are specifically linked to publishers. Therefore, you may not resell your ISBNs to someone else who will publish them under their own name or a different publishing entity. You can purchase your ISBN by going directly to **myidentifiers.com**.

For a lower cost, Amazon services makes ISBNs available to people who publish through them. While that may save you money, it also means that Amazon will be listed as the publisher. Some people do not want that, as it makes it apparent that the book is being self-published. While self-publishing is gaining in respect, many authors prefer to publish under their own name or publishing company to maintain tighter control of their product and pursue their own brand and publishing. They also feel it makes them appear more professional to their readers.

When considering ISBNs, you should be aware that a separate ISBN is needed for each version of a book. You do not need a new ISBN if you simply make a few minor edits to your book. However, a paperback and a hardback of the same book each require a separate ISBN, as does an e-book and a large print version. In the case where you anticipate having several versions of the same book, the cost of multiple ISBNs may become important.

Copyright

Copyright is a gray area in writing and many authors disagree about the importance of obtaining a specific, legal copyright for their work. Essentially, once you have written a work and saved it, it is yours. You have copyrighted it simply by doing that.

There is an additional copyright, however, that can be done through the legal system. This is referred to as **copyright registration**. That process registers your work publicly as being copyrighted. Many people consider this process to be "enhanced" protection for your work. Many authors insist on doing this copyright registration. Other writers rely on the fact that they have saved and published their work as adequate copyright.

The major benefit of copyright registration is that if you end up suing someone for plagiarizing your work, it may be easier for you to receive monetary reimbursement for damages through the courts. If you doubt you will need to sue someone for damages, this may not be an important issue for you.

Specifically, the U.S. Copyright Office advises that our work is copyrighted the moment it is created in a tangible form, either directly or with the aid of a machine or device. In other words, your manuscript can be written out by hand, typed, or saved electronically to have copyright protection without the work being officially registered through the U.S. Copyright Office.

Here are some relevant FAQs from the U.S. Copyright Office website to consider.

- Do I have to register with your office to be protected?

No. In general, registration is voluntary. Copyright exists from the moment the work is created. You will have to register, however, if you wish to bring a lawsuit for infringement of a U.S. work. See Circular 1, Copyright Basics, section "Copyright Registration."

- Why should I register my work if copyright protection is automatic?

Registration is recommended for a number of reasons. Many choose to register their works because they wish to have the facts of their copyright on the public record and have a certificate of registration. Registered works may be eligible for statutory damages and attorney's fees in successful litigation. Finally, if registration occurs within five years of publication, it is considered *prima facie* evidence in a court of law. See Circular 1, Copyright Basics, section "Copyright Registration" and Circular 38b, Highlights of Copyright

Amendments Contained in the Uruguay Round Agreements Act (URAA), on non-U.S. works.

Here is the link to the form to copyright literary material directly with the U.S. Copyright Office: copyright.gov/forms/formtx.pdf.

There are many companies that will assist you in formally copyrighting your work for an additional fee.

Bar Codes

Bar codes are an additional requirement for printed books. Some companies will create bar codes for your book for a fee. If you purchase a bar code from one of those companies, you must then make sure it is located on the book cover you provide to Amazon. Be sure also to check the box on the upload page that you are providing your own bar code.

The bar code goes at the bottom right corner of your book's back cover. Your purchased bar code will be provided to you in a form that will allow you to simply place it into your book cover file. Then you save the entire file as a PDF, ready to upload to KDP.

If you do not provide a bar code on your book cover, however, simply do not check the box on the upload page. Amazon will create and place a bar code on your back cover for you.

The cost for a company, such as Bowker Identifier to create a bar code for your book is very little—generally about $5.00. There is little reason however to pay for this as Amazon's bar code is free and does not affect your publishing rights. If you remove your book from publication through Amazon and publish elsewhere, however, you will be required to remove the Amazon barcode and use a new one. In that event, either your new publisher will provide one for you or you may then purchase one elsewhere.

Other Legalities

With all aspects of publishing, make sure you have proper permissions and licenses to use photographs, illustrations, and software in your book. You need to not just have general permission; you need to have permission and license to use those things for commercial use.

You are publishing a book to sell. Whether you make oodles of money or practically nothing is not the relevant point. If you are publishing a book to sell, you are using those photographs, illustrations, and software in a commercial application. You must therefore make sure you have the proper licensing or permissions.

ISBN, copyright, bar codes, permission, and licensing are legal hoops to jump through. Fortunately, the hoops are low to the ground, inexpensive, and do not require too much time or effort. That gives us time to start the next step in book production, selecting the physical material that will make up our printed book.

Time to determine the legal information
for your book. Do you have that information handy
or do you need to obtain it?

Checklist

☐ My ISBN for this book is: _____

☐ I want/do not want to register my copyright.

☐ If so, I registered my copyright on _____.

☐ I will/will not place a bar code on my back cover.

☐ I need appropriate permissions/licenses for:

_____

Chapter 6

What is Your Book Made of?

Cover Material

While your book's cover is not technically part of what is inside the cover, selecting the material on which it will be printed relates to the physical aspect of your book, including what is inside. Your cover material affects the feel of the book when your reader picks it up. The cover is not just about the image on the front of the book. A printed book cover involves both visual and touch sensations.

Independently published authors generally have two choices for their cover material: glossy or matt. Some authors believe this should simply be a matter of choice. But there are other things to consider.

As with most aspects of book production, there are traditional standards within the publishing world. While those standards are changing and are less widely adopted by independent publishers, they still exist. It is worth knowing what those standards are to help you choose the material for your own book.

What is Your Book Made of?

Traditionally, non-fiction books use a matt finish for covers. Glossy covers are reserved for fiction and children's books. Sometimes however, an author might select a different material for a specific reason. Here are a few ideas to help you think through the idea of using a material that is not standard in the publishing industry.

- Matt covers have a soft texture to the touch. They therefore might suggest femininity. You might consider using a matt finish for a romance novel or a novel about grief or emotional pain.

- Similarly, the soft texture of matt covers might be a good choice for a non-fiction book on a sensitive matter, such as grief or a book on helping aging parents or special-needs children.

- Glossy covers appear more vibrant, whereas matt covers slightly dull the artwork—which can be very effective for certain genres and themes, but not for others.

- Matt covers tend to be more scratch resistant. Some authors therefore like to use them for children's books that will get more wear.

- Glossy covers, on the other hand, are more attractive to children. Therefore, you would want to weigh the importance of attractiveness vs. durability.

- A humorous non-fiction book with a super fun cover image might lend itself more to a glossy cover.

In addition to matt and glossy, some print-on-demand publishers offer hardcover or hardcover plus book jacket. Some publishers also offer embossed covers or covers with metallic medallions. Materials used for children's book covers are limited only by imagination and cost.

Covers can be created using a variety of materials. For most independent authors, we can select either matt or glossy. There are industry standards that should guide our selection, but as with everything, once you know the rule and have clear reasons for doing so, feel free to break it.

Paper

At the same time you are selecting the cover material during the production of your book on KDP, you will also select the paper for the book's interior. Your choices are cream or white.

Cream paper can only be used with black print inside. That means, any graphs, photographs, or illustrations you want to include inside the book must be black or grayscale. Color images will be affected by the cream-colored background. Therefore, if you plan to have color inside your book, your choice is white.

Additionally, the cream paper tends to be more porous than white. That means black and grayscale graphics could potentially be slightly less crisp. Keep that in mind also, when selecting which paper for your book's interior.

Additionally, cream paper is that it is thicker than white. By mistake, I once set up a middle grade fiction book on cream paper. I created the book cover, however, for white paper. I sized the book cover properly for white paper at 12.680" x 9.250". The cover was unacceptable to Amazon, because for cream paper, it needed to be 12.727" wide. That is a difference of .47 inches; nearly ½ inch for the cover width.

Some reasons why you might want to use cream paper include:

- Because it is thicker, cream paper will give your book a heftier feel. If your book is "slight" in length, using a thicker paper will make the book feel more substantial. It will give your buyer a sense of value.

- Another reason you might want to use cream paper is because it gives the interior a sense of the old world. If your book is a historical fiction, historical romance, high fantasy or even a non-fiction book about a time or place in antiquity, using cream paper can help accentuate the overall theme of the book.

- Using cream paper, however, adds cost to the book. You will therefore need to pass that cost on to the buyer in the form of a higher price. Or you will need to reduce the amount of royalty you earn on each book.

- White paper on the other hand costs less and therefore either the price to your buyer can be lower or your profit can be higher. White paper is also smoother to the touch and looks and feels crisp and clean.

- Additionally, if you have any colored photos, illustrations, or graphs or charts inside your book, Amazon will require you to use white paper. White paper, however, will make all your photos or illustrations cleaner, even if they do not include color. The text itself will also appear crisper, making it easier on your reader's eyes. White paper is therefore an excellent choice for most books unless you specifically want the cream paper choice to accentuate your theme.

What is Your Book Made of?

One caution you should be aware of as it relates to paper is that once you publish your book through Amazon KDP, you cannot change the paper choice. If you absolutely must change your book's interior paper, you will need a new ISBN. That can add to your production cost.

It is time to select the material you want
for the cover and interior paper of your book.

Checklist

☐ The cover material I want for this book is matt/glossy
_____.

☐ I have color illustrations or grayscale photos/graphics that require white paper for my interior _____.

☐ The paper for my interior will be _____.

Chapter 7

Chapter Titles and Subheadings

Titles and subtitles are there to help our reader. Chapters in novels help readers break down story and separate scenes. Chapters in nonfiction help organize information so readers can more easily assimilate it. In all cases, titles and subtitles are there to help our readers make sense of our books and to keep them reading to the end.

By the time you have finished writing your book, you will have broken it down into appropriate chapters. Now is the time to look at those chapters and subchapters and help the reader further by creating helpful visual cues.

Chapter Numbers

In all things relating to book headings, it is critical to always keep things consistent. If you start in chapter one by numbering it...

Chapter One: Title

...then don't start the next chapter with

Chapter Titles and Subheadings

Chapter 2—Title

Keep the structure of your titles consistent throughout the book.

Possibilities for chapter titles include:

- Number chapters as 1, 2, 3 or One, Two, Three or I, II, III

- Or you may decide not to number chapters; just have a title

- Or you may choose to use both a number and a title—either both on the same line or Chapter + Number on one line and title on the next (single spaced) like this:

Chapter One

Chapter Title

Here is what my **Style** looks like for the creation of my chapter titles. You will note that I need two separate Styles for each chapter: one for the Chapter + number and a second Style for the chapter title. You may initially plan to have your Chapter number and title on one line. Sometimes, however, chapter titles wrap onto the next line. A separate style for the chapter title makes sure things are consistent.

Remember that your version of Microsoft Word or your screen's customization or configuration may appear different than mine.

Style for Chapter title (Chapter + number). First click on the A+ to create a new Style as before. Set your initial Style name and format the font type and size. I used Cambria 16 bold, centered.

Click on the Format box at the bottom of the dialogue box and open Paragraph. Then add the number of spaces before the chapter title and between the chapter title and subtitle (or text).

Chapter Titles and Subheadings

Paragraph ? ✕

Indents and Spacing   Line and Page Breaks

General

Alignment: Centered

Outline level: Body Text   ☐ Collapsed by default

Indentation

Left: 0"   Special: By:

Right: 0"   (none)

☐ Mirror indents

Spacing

Before: 144 pt   Line spacing: At:

After: 12 pt   Single

☐ Don't add space between paragraphs of the same style

Preview

Tabs...   Set As Default   OK   Cancel

You can see that I have set the spacing for 144 pt before my chapter + number. There is then 12 pt after that and before the chapter title (or first line of text).

Here is how I set up the chapter style for the name of the chapter. I selected Cambria, size 16, centered bold. Opening the Format box, I entered 12 pt above and 18 pt below the subtitle and single spaced if my subtitle is lengthy and the text must wrap to the next line.

Chapter Titles and Subheadings

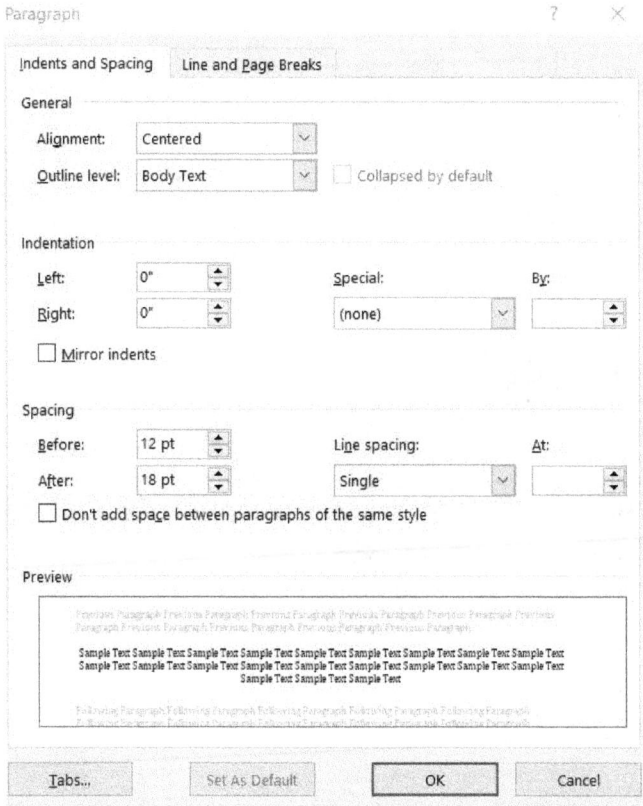

Keep the font style and size consistent throughout your book also. If the title for chapter one is in Cambria bold size 16, make sure all chapter titles are Cambria bold size 16. Also make sure the spacing before the chapter title is the same for all chapters. And make sure the spacing between the chapter title and the first paragraph are the same for all chapters. And make sure all chapters begin on odd pages and have no headers or page numbers (more on these rules later).

Subheadings for text

When it comes to subheadings for non-fiction, the rule is: use enough subheadings for clarity but not so many that the information feels busy. Additionally, if you break down a subsection and it contains only a sentence or two, that point may not be perceived as important or persuasive by your reader. Instead, you can either expand the information or include it within another, related subsection.

Titles are generally centered and in larger, bold font. Subheadings can be either centered or left justified.

Proper Section Numbering

For headings and all interior content that requires numbering, make sure to follow proper standardization sequencing. This may depend on which **style guide** you use on a regular basis. The following is based on the **MLA Style Manual**. You will recognize it from your grammar school days.

- Roman numerals: I, II, III
    - Capital letters: A, B, C
        - Arabic numerals (no parentheses): 1, 2, 3
            - Small letters: a, b, c (no parentheses)

That is probably as far down on an outline format as you will want to go in your chapter subsections. But for easy reference, after small letters without parentheses, it continues with Arabic numerals in parentheses or half parentheses, then small Roman numerals in parentheses or half parentheses.

Chapter Titles and Subheadings

When you begin using an outlining format for your subsections, you may have to reconfigure the default in your Microsoft Word file. Microsoft uses its own **Microsoft Style Guide** as its default. The Microsoft Style Guide has been set up for many diverse uses. It is therefore quite dissimilar to standard style guides for writing and publishing. Since, as authors, we strive to be seen as professional within the book publishing industry, it is best for us to follow standard style guides, regardless of what Microsoft wants us to do.

Always, always, always, however, remember that if you have a point A in your writing, you must also have at least a point B. If you have a subsection 1, you must also have at least a subsection 2. If you only have a single subpoint, it should either be expanded, deleted, or incorporated within another subsection or within the main section itself.

The biggest point to remember for chapter titles and subheadings is consistency. That is another beauty of using **Styles**. Once you have decided on exactly how you want your titles and subheadings to be displayed, a click of the mouse will make sure they are consistent each time you need them to be.

It is time to decide on the look
of your book's chapter titles and subheadings.
It is worth the effort.

Checklist

☐ The chapter titles for my book will look like this:

Chapter Titles and Subheadings

Font style: _____

Font size: _____

Bold/No Bold: _____

Placement of chapter number and subtitle:

_____

☐ I have established a Style(s) for my chapter titles.

Chapter 8

Visual Cues for Multiple POV

One issue many novelists encounter is how to visually cue their reader when the story switches **point of view (POV)**. Certainly, a well-defined voice for different characters is helpful, but sometimes readers still need to be alerted when the story moves to a different time or place or character. Visual cues are helpful.

The number one recommendation by fiction editors is to give each character a new chapter or section when the story switches to their point of view. Some authors who begin a new chapter with that character, simply name the chapter with that character's name.

Of course, having chapters alternately titled Samantha and Michael makes a table of contents that lists chapter titles of little value. But that style of titling can nonetheless be helpful in letting the reader know whose head we are presently inside.

Sometimes, an author will switch POVs within a chapter. There are several common visual cues that authors use to alert their readers to this switch. One visual cue used is to simply end that character's story at the end of the paragraph. The author will format the text with a blank line. Next will be a series of asterisks or another symbol, centered on the page. There will be a second blank line, followed by the text written in the new POV starting with the next paragraph. Like this:

I can't wait to see Michael and know what he thinks of my new plan. Samantha hugged herself and spun in a circle. "Michael!" she whispered.

***

Samantha sounds excited. Maybe I should cancel our date. I can't face her high-strung emotions right now.

In a similar way, some authors simply leave two or three blank lines between character points of view. The danger with that formatting, of course, is that your POV switch might occur at the end of a page. When that happens, the reader does not have a visual cue to alert her to the POV change.

Other writers like to show POV change by using a different font for each character. You might use a *serif* font, for example for a female protagonist and a *sans serif* font for a male protagonist (more about fonts in Chapter 9). If you use different fonts, of course you must be diligent in consistently using the appropriate font for the appropriate character. Additionally, if you have many points of view and therefore use many different style fonts, you run the risk of visually irritating your reader with countless things they need to keep track of.

A *serif* font, handwriting font or italics are often used for memories, journal entries, ghosts, or spiritual beings. They may also be used when quoting Scripture, poems, or other published works for both novels and nonfiction books. Keep in mind that if the same font for the new POV as is used for the rest of the manuscript, simply italicizing it gives the reader a visual cue that something is different.

However you decide to handle change of point of view, do so consistently. Remember that the physical book you are creating can give your readers additional cues to help them understand your book without expending additional effort on their part. Experiment with how using font styles or formatting the text on the printed (or electronic) page can visually help your readers love your book.

Think through your book.
Do you have multiple points of view?
Do you want to set off portions of your text,
for such things as quotes from other sources?

Checklist

☐ I have the following points of view for my novel:

_____

_____

_____

_____

☐ I will include the quotations, poems, or other text that might be set off to visually cue the reader: _____

Visual Cues for Multiple POV

☐ I will do the following to visually cue my reader:

_____

_____

_____

Chapter 9

Fonts

In the last chapter we saw how using different fonts can visually alert your reader to a change of point of view. Because the words you have written must be displayed visually, the fonts you select can be a valuable visual element of your book.

Microsoft Word provides dozens of fonts for us to choose from. Additionally, we can download hundreds more. While some fonts may be similar, often one will jump off the screen and sit triumphantly on the printed page.

But the decision on which font to use should be made on purpose. The visual impact of an individual font has a lot to do with what your reader will associate it with.

Size

As with most things having to do with book publication, there are size standards within the publishing industry. Part of the choice as to font size has to do with our reader. We therefore need to understand who our reader is.

Fonts

Generally, for YA and adult readers, whether fiction or non-fiction, the industry standard is size 10-point (often abbreviated as pt) font. Readers over 50 who are getting used to wearing glasses, appreciate a slightly larger print. Size 12-point font is a good choice for them. For children under 12 who are just learning to read, a size 12-point font also is a good choice, allowing adequate white space on the page so they can focus on one word at a time.

Large print books are considered large print if the font is 16-point or larger. Be aware that if you have a regular version of a book and a large print version, you will need two individual ISBNs—one for each version. You are then able, however, to label the one "large print version" and gain extra marketability for your work with readers looking for large print books to enjoy.

Font Type

Consider also font type. Think about how the look of your font relates to your particular book—your genre, your theme, your content. Most fonts are divided into two types: *serif* and *sans serif.*

Serif Fonts

A *serif* is the little tag on the ends of upright parts of letters. It is a French word meaning

> *any of the short lines stemming from and at an angle to the upper and lower ends of the strokes of a letter* (Meriam-webster.com).

Here are a few examples of *serif* fonts:

Fonts

Cambria (used in this book)

Georgia

Times New Roman

Sagona Book

Note that all of the above *serif* fonts are in size 12 point, yet the size varies between them. The reasoning is because the point size is measured in height. Therefore, all of the above are the same point size in height, even though Sagona Book is much wider and thus appears larger than Times New Roman.

Serif fonts evoke a sense of femininity, tradition, history, faith, and Old World. They are therefore good choices for many novels, inspirational or historical books, and many books for women on a variety of subjects.

Sans Serif Fonts

Sans serif is French for *without serif.* In other words, a *sans serif* font is one without the little tags.

Here are a few examples of *sans serif* fonts:

Arial

Calibri

Tahoma

Verdana

Fonts

Note that all of the above *sans serif* fonts are in size 12-point, and not bolded, although they may appear to be because of the thickness of the font.

Sans serif fonts tend to look clean and modern. They are therefore often a good choice for non-fiction books, especially about technology, medicine, health, science, engineering, or anything that may require a complex explanation. They are a good choice for science fiction books. They also subtly evoke a more masculine sense that may appeal to men.

In addition to the general categories of font styles of *serif* and *sans serif*, are specialty styles, such as

ALGERIAN

Brush Script MT

Bradley Hand ITC

Chiller

Again, note that all the above fonts are in size 12-point. There is an obvious size appearance between Algerian and Chiller, even though the selection is the same size (height) for both.

Naturally, you would not use one of these specialty styles for the complete text of your book because they make reading visually difficult for your reader. But you might decide to use one for a single quote, a poem, or title. Just experiment with fonts to see what they look like, what emotions or themes they evoke and whether one might visually accentuate or enhance your book.

Branding

In addition to enhancing the look of your particular book, consider the effect a specific font style might have on your writing brand. Certain authors will select one specific font, for example, for their name (and sometimes the title) for all their books. The font reflects the genre they write and who they are as a writer. To a certain extent, the style font they select *becomes* part of their brand. When a reader picks up one of their books, they recognize the author's name in part because of the font used. It is part of visual recognition of the author's brand.

This writing brand can continue inside the book as well. For example, part of my writing brand is that I am a traditional person—in my values, in what I write about, and in how I present myself. I don't feel comfortable with anything flashy. I don't want to be perceived as outside the norm. I therefore have chosen Cambria font as my preferred font. I use it in my novels. I use it in my non-fiction books on writing. I use it in my Bible studies and inspirational writing. The specific Cambria font has become part of my writing brand.

What that means for this book, is that I have consciously chosen to use a *serif* font instead of a *sans serif* font that is often typically used for nonfiction books. While, the cover uses a *sans serif* font for the title, my name, as in most of my book covers, is typed in the *serif* font Cambria.

As you select the font for your books, therefore, consider how the font might reinforce or accentuate your writing brand. If you write in widely diverse genres maybe this is not something for you to consider. Instead, you might focus on how a specific font style (and size) might visually enhance each particular book.

Fonts

Be proactive about the font you select. There are thousands of great ones available. Pick one you and your readers will love.

> The font you select for your book interior can reflect your book's genre, its theme, and even your brand as a writer. It is time to decide on purpose which font you will use for your book.

Checklist

☐ My book's genre or theme: _____

☐ The font that best supports my brand as a writer is:

_____

☐ The font I have selected for my book's interior is:

_____

Chapter 10

Chapter Beginnings

Earlier we talked about chapter titles. The topic of chapter beginnings is something entirely different. It is also something that can be fun for and helpful for your reader.

Formatting

The standard in the publishing industry is to always begin the first page of a chapter on the right-hand side of the book (as I have done in this book). We say that chapters begin on odd-numbered pages.

In reality, however, the standard in the publishing industry is that the first pages of chapters are not numbered. Imagine an invisible number on chapter title pages instead. It is included within the numbering of the book as a whole; we just don't see it on the page.

Look at the bottom of this page. There is no number. The pagination continues properly from the previous page number to the number on the next page, however. Where a page is blank, that page is also included within the book's overall pagination, except that blank pages are not numbered either—except in invisible ink.

In other words, chapters begin on the right-hand side of the page. One result of that book layout is that you may then have a blank page on the left-hand side of the book facing the new chapter page. If your previous chapter ends on an odd numbered page and the new chapter begins on the next invisibly odd numbered page, you will have a blank page between them. That is industry standard. It is what your readers expect. It gives them comfort when your book does that.

Occasionally, an author will try to save money on the production cost of a book by ignoring this rule and having no blank pages. They therefore begin a new chapter on whatever page is next. If your book is lengthy, you may decide to do this on purpose to save pages and therefore save cost. If you do so, keep it consistent. Although readers expect chapters to always begin on odd-numbered pages, they will ultimately accept it if you do not—as long as you keep the formatting consistent throughout the book.

Additionally, industry standard is that first pages of chapters have no headings. Blank pages on the left side of the book have no numbers or headings either. These are industry standards in book production.

"Wait," you say. You said, "chapter beginnings can be fun."

Yes! They can. They can effectively enhance the theme and visual feel of your entire book.

Beginning Flash

There are many ways you can make your chapter beginnings stand out. Earlier we discussed the various ways to format your chapter numbers and titles (see Chapter 7). Now is the time to ramp it up visually. Let's first talk about the beginnings of the first paragraph in each chapter.

Industry standard for all chapter beginnings is that the first line of the first paragraph of chapters is not indented. Regardless of whether you indent the first lines of your subsequent paragraphs or double space between paragraphs, industry standard says that first lines are *not indented.* So, before we even look at other fun formatting, the industry standard for chapter beginnings makes beginnings interesting for readers. They are also a visual cue: chapter beginnings signal something new is coming.

One way authors can visually enhance their manuscript is by using **dropped capitals** for that first line of first paragraphs. A dropped cap basically increases the size of the first letter in the first word of the first paragraph of each chapter and drops it below the line of text. The effect visually is that it adds an element of tradition. It feels Old World. There is a visual sense of romance and history. A dropped cap subtly reminds readers of illuminated manuscripts such as elegant Bible translations intricately illustrated by Old World monks.

You would probably not use a dropped cap for a nonfiction book about engineering a space shuttle. But it might work well for a historical fiction, an inspirational story, or a memoir with a theme of faith.

Here is how to create a dropped cap in Microsoft Word. Remember that your version of Word or your screen's customization or configuration may be different from mine.

- Type your text. Then highlight the first letter you want to drop by left clicking before the letter, holding the click and moving the mouse right to highlight the letter. Release the mouse click.

- Go to the **Insert** tab on the Ribbon. Move to the far right and click on the icon of the **Capital A** with three short lines and one long line. A drop-down menu will open. Select and left click on **Dropped**.

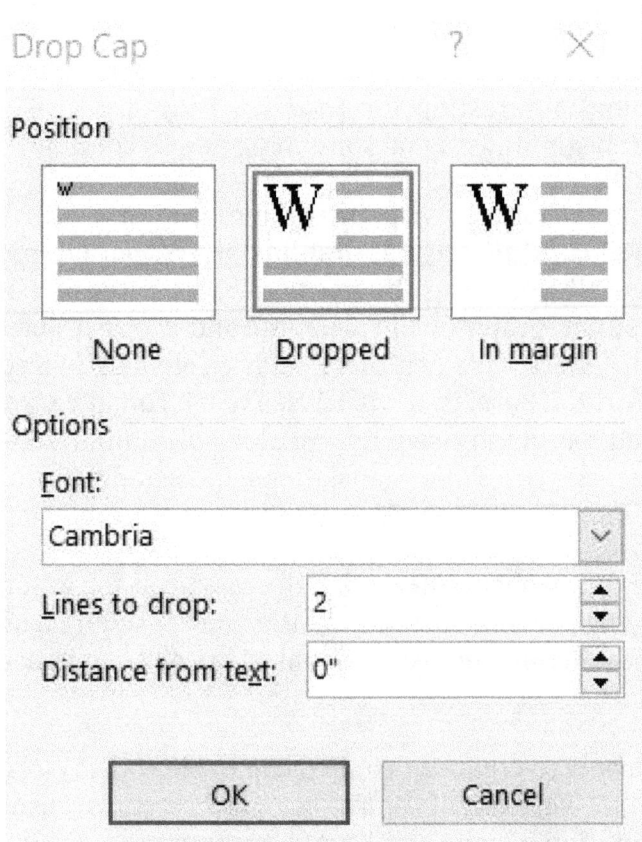

The default is that the first letter in that paragraph will be turned into a 3-line dropped cap. If you want a dropped cap of fewer or more lines, select **Drop Cap Options**. A new dialogue box will open and allow you to indicate how many lines you want to drop. Would you like to see what this looks like?

H ere is a dropped cap with two lines. Here is a dropped cap with two lines. Here is a dropped cap with two lines. Here is a dropped cap with two lines.

H ere is a dropped cap with three lines. Here is a dropped cap with three lines. Here is a dropped cap with three lines. Here is a dropped cap with three lines. Here is a dropped cap with three lines. Here is a dropped cap with three lines.

Another way to make your chapter beginning stand out is to choose a unique font style for your first word or two.

FOR EXAMPLE, the main text of this book uses Cambria; here the first two words are in Castellar font.

ANOTHER WAY SOME AUTHORS SET OFF their chapter beginnings is to type the first six words of a chapter in all caps, like I have done in this paragraph.

Whether you choose one of these ideas or simply set off your chapter beginning by not indenting that first line, keep in mind that chapter beginnings are important. They signal that something new is about to happen. "Readers, pay attention," they say.

Give your readers a visual signal to help them prepare for the good stuff to come. Then keep it consistent throughout your book.

Paragraph Beginnings

In addition to chapter beginnings, you have a choice about how to begin the other paragraphs in your manuscript.

We have seen that publishing industry standard is to have the first line of each chapter left justified; without indentation. Even if you indent subsequent paragraphs in your manuscript, the very first line of the very first paragraph of each chapter should be left justified. In other words, regardless of what you do in the rest of your manuscript, that first line should not be indented.

The rest of the paragraphs—whether to indent or not—is up to you. But as with all things, you should consider the visual aspect of indentation. You should also consider your brand. Additionally, you should consider the industry standards for your specific genre.

Yes, genres often vary on the issue of indenting vs. double spacing between paragraphs. In general, romance novels, books for women readers, and more traditional books will indent paragraphs. Indented paragraphs give a softer, more conventional, old fashioned visual appearance to the page.

On the other hand, nonfiction, topics about modern life, technology, science, or engineering tend to double space between paragraphs. Visually, the look is cleaner, less visually fussy.

For children also, more white space on the page provided by double spacing between paragraphs, helps early readers focus on the words and sentences they may be struggling with. In a similar way, for books that are heavy on facts, statistics, or science and technology, extra white space allows the reader time and room between words to assimilate tougher information without undue eye or brain strain.

Double spacing between paragraphs also gives a modern or futuristic look to science fiction novels. Men also tend to like the cleaner look of double-spaced paragraphs.

In other words, think about what your book contains and your specific reader. Think about which formatting layout might best benefit both, as well as enhancing your personal writing brand.

As a side note, double spacing between paragraphs tends to lengthen a manuscript, potentially adding pages to it over only indenting the first lines. This will be a benefit to you if you feel the overall book length needs some "padding." That idea is not meant to deceive your reader by adding length without adding content. Your reader, however, may feel like she is getting more value for her money if the book feels adequate in length.

Conversely, if your book is already lengthy, adding more pages will by necessity add cost to your book. Switching to indented paragraphs might allow you to lower the cost to your buyer or increase the profit to you.

◆◆◆

There are many reasons to determine whether to indent or double space your book interior. Make sure you look at them all, most especially how the formatting affects the visual style of your book interior and helps your reader love your book.

Formatting of pages gives your book a unique feel and visual element. It is therefore valuable to consider the layout of chapter beginnings and subsequent paragraphs.

Chapter Beginnings

Checklist

☐ Look at the options available to you for the first line of each chapter: Left justified only, dropped capital, unique font for first word or phrase, capitalize first six words. I choose the following:

_____

☐ I choose to left justify or indent first line of all subsequent paragraphs in my interior because:

_____

_____

Chapter 11

Pagination

My biggest struggle in book production is pagination. How is it possible for itty bitty numbers which sit all by themselves on the page to cause so much trouble?

What Gets Numbered?

We talked about numbering pages back in the last chapter when we mentioned the industry standard that there are no numbers shown on the first page of new chapters. There are also no numbers on blank pages at the left-hand side of the book preceding the first page of new chapters. Those pages are included within the total numbering of the book; they just do not show up on the physical page. We might imagine they are written in invisible ink.

In addition to those pages that are unnumbered, we also do not include the front matter and back matter of our books within our book numbering. Decades past, the pages in front and back matter were sometimes numbered using a lower-case Roman numeral system. That is no longer the industry standard. Now, those pages are simply left unnumbered. We will cover front and back matter later.

Pagination, by industry standard, now begins on page one of our book's interior with an invisible number 1. The first number on a page we see is on page two.

In addition, Section and Part break pages are included within the numbering. They too, however, are left with invisible numbers.

Location for Pagination

Microsoft Word offers you many options for placement of page numbers. But many of those locations are not appropriate for books. Still, click through the options to become familiar with your choices. Look also at books in your genre written by other authors. See what choice their publisher has selected. Think whether that choice might be appropriate for your book.

Some authors prefer page numbers to be on the upper outside corner of pages. Some authors prefer the lower outside corner of pages. Some prefer the bottom center of the page. The simplest placement from a technical point of view is bottom center. That allows for less clutter in the header at the top of the page. (Headers will be covered in the next chapter). It is also technically simpler to implement because the placement will be centered on the page whether that page is odd or even numbered.

MY WARNING: I have published over 24 books using Amazon publishing—both when it was Createspace and now under KDP. It is only for the last half dozen books that I have not ended in tears at some point during the pagination process. I love technology when it does what I think it should. I hate it when it doesn't. But through it all is an underlying truth: it only does what I have told it to do.

Therefore, when Microsoft Word does something I didn't want it to do or does it in a way I didn't intend, it is my fault for giving it incorrect instructions. My bad.

I share this as encouragement. You can do it. Just take things step-by-step. If it doesn't work properly, review each step you took until you find what you told Microsoft Word to do wrong. Then change it.

Steps in Pagination

Here is the simplest way I know to paginate your manuscript. This will result in page numbers at the bottom center of each page, except, of course, for first pages of chapters and blank pages. It begins the pagination with an invisible page one on the first page of Chapter One and each subsequent chapter. Numbers appear beginning on page two.

Remember that your version of Microsoft Word or your screen's customization or configuration may be different from mine.

- Choose the page of your document where you want to start numbering from (the first page of Chapter 1). Before starting your pagination, make sure the **Link to Previous** is not highlighted. Make sure the **Different First Page** box is checked so that no page number will appear on the first page of each chapter.

- Navigate the cursor to the beginning of page one and click **Insert→Page Number.** Choose the style of page number you want and where on the page you want it placed.

- If you don't want a page number to appear on the first page (you don't), click on **Different First Page.**

- Go to **Page Number→Format Page Numbers**. Set it to start at 1.

At this point, Word will place an "invisible" number 1 on the first page. Then **Close Header and Footer.**

Once closed, your book should now be paginated.

Troubleshooting Pagination

If you go through your manuscript and find that page numbers are not consistent, the following are typical problems to check for.

Pagination

Is Link to Previous highlighted or not highlighted? You want it **not highlighted** right at the point where you begin your pagination. You **do want it highlighted** for the rest of your pages, until you reach your back matter. At that point, you want the link **not highlighted again** to tell Word to stop paginating. If these are properly highlighted, you may need to delete any odd page numbers before page 1 and before your back matter.

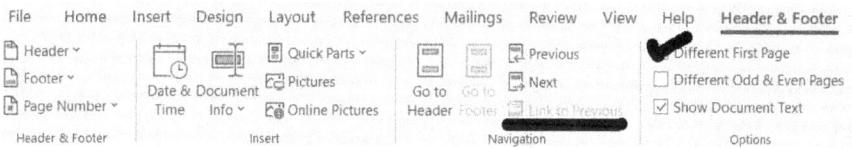

Check also that you have selected Different First Page so that chapter beginnings will not paginate.

You might also need to check the section breaks in your document. Check especially the section breaks at beginnings of chapters. Section breaks are instructions to tell Word where you want things—like pagination—to happen. We don't need to understand how it all works, just that it does what we tell it to do. We need to tell it to continue to do something (pagination) or stop doing something (headers) by way of choosing to Link to Previous or not.

Link to Previous, the Different First Page box, and Section Breaks are the keys to proper pagination. Incorrect use of them is usually the trouble when proper pagination fails.

You should now see that all your pages, including the first ones, are numbered. If you struggle with pagination and think the issue of breaks may be your problem, click on the **Paragraph Icon** on the Ribbon.

Pagination

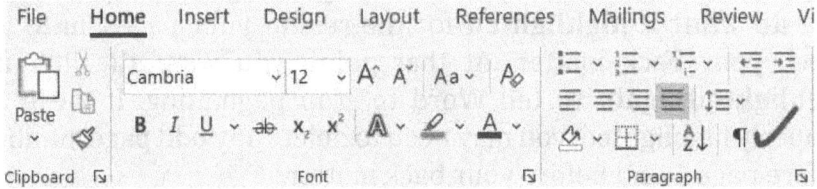

All spaces, punctuation, and other technical instructions then become visible. Your text will generally appear like this:

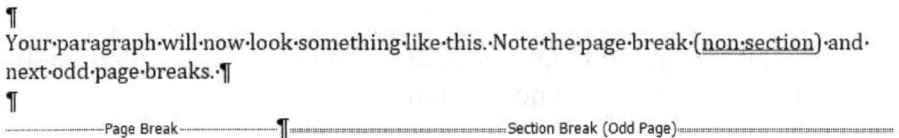

¶
Your·paragraph·will·now·look·something·like·this.·Note·the·page·break·(non·section)·and· next·odd·page·breaks.·¶
¶
----------Page Break----------¶ ==============Section Break (Odd Page)==============

Clicking on the **Paragraph Icon** will also tell you whether the break you inserted is the proper one. If not, your pagination and headers may not format properly.

That's when the crying begins for me. If you struggle with pagination and breaks, I urge you to watch tutorials and read instructions about how to use them in your Microsoft Word document. Or plan to have extra boxes of tissues handy and plenty of coffee to get you through.

Good luck!

Your Word document software will do exactly what
you have told it to do. Problems occur when we
have told it to do something in a way that is
not what we planned.

Checklist

☐ The location to paginate my interior will be:

_____

☐ The font type and size will be: _____

Chapter 12

Headers

Headers in books are those lines of information at the top of each page. They remind the reader what they are reading. Not all genres have headers as standard practices in publishing, but many do. There are also variations for placement and content in headers. Part of that is personal preference; part is what information you deem most important to remind the reader without overloading them or visually distracting them from the main body of text.

As you think about headers for your book, remember that any text you have at the top (or bottom) of the page adds visual complexity for your reader. You do not want to clutter the page visually. You just want to provide enough information to help your reader.

As mentioned, not all genres include headers. Early readers for children, for example, do not. They simply have page numbers, located away from text so the text is clearly separated from everything else. A header in an early reader would confuse a child who might turn a page and begin reading the header instead of the next line of the story's text.

Book Title and Chapter Title

The traditional standard for headers in publishing nonfiction is to place the book title on the left-hand page; the chapter title on the right with the book seam in the center. Like this:

Inside the Covers   Headers
(left hand page)   (center seam)   (right hand page)

You can also decide if you want each header justified at the outside edge of the paper or centered on the page. In addition, decide if you want the headers to be in upper/lower case or all caps. You might decide to use a different font for your headers. In fact, you will probably need to reformat the font for your headers, because Microsoft will have previously given them a default font style and size. You can easily change those in the drop down **Modify** box.

Other Formats for Headers

Some fiction authors prefer to put their last name on the right-hand page and the chapter title on the left. Like this:

Headers   (center seam)   Peterson

Other authors put the chapter title on both sides, like I have done in this book, regardless of whether it is fiction or nonfiction. I prefer this choice because I assume that if a person is reading the book, they know its title. Although I hope they remember my name, I feel it is more important for a nonfiction book that I provide information to help them as they are reading. Having the chapter title on both pages makes it particularly easy for readers to know where they are in the book. That is the reasoning behind this choice.

Another reason you might have for selecting a header that is the same on both sides of the page, is that it is technologically simpler. As with pagination, the issue of headers has to do with page and section breaks, along with making sure to link and unlink sections on each and every page of your manuscript. The fewer times you are required to tell Microsoft to do that, the easier it will be for you to create consistent headers.

How to Format the Headers in This Book

Here are the steps to take to achieve the headers I use in this book—with the chapter title centered on all pages (except of course the first page of each chapter and blank pages).

Remember that your version of Microsoft Word or your screen's customization or configuration may be different from mine.

Go to the Ribbon. Click on **Insert**; then **Header**.

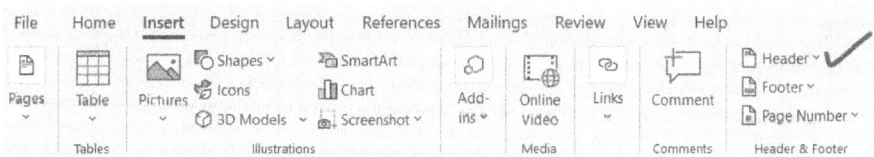

Open the dialogue box under **Header** and select the header type you prefer. We will select **Blank**. Notice that the location for text is set at the left-hand side of the blank header. We want the text to be centered. To do so, go to the **Home** tab on the Ribbon and click on the centered text within the **Paragraph** section.

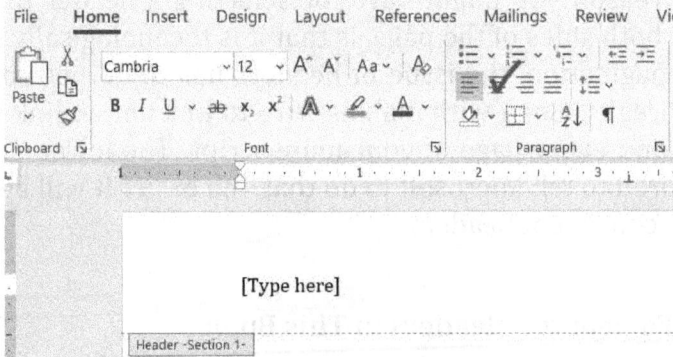

Then when you type in the title of your book, it will center it on the page. Like this:

When you are done, simply click the big red X to close the **Header and Footer** box.

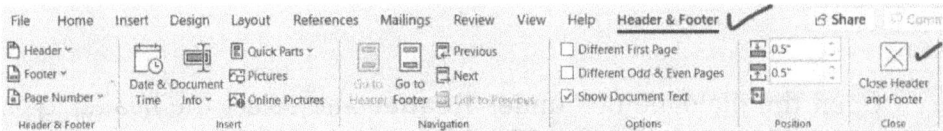

If you decide to change the font for your headers—either to set them off or to change the Microsoft default to match your interior, here is what you do.

After you have typed in the header text you desire, go to the **Home** tab on the Ribbon. Click on the font box and select the style and font you desire. Enter. You should now have your desired font for your header.

Troubleshooting Headers

Placement and content of headers can be technically tricky. The key, as with pagination, is the placement and type of section breaks that you have included within your text. If you have trouble getting your headers to appear as you want, the first step is to go to the **Home** tab and click on the **paragraph icon**. Check what types of **breaks** you have inserted. Check also to make sure the **Link to Previous** choice on the **Header and Footer** navigation tab is properly selected.

If you have selected Link to Previous, Microsoft Word will link the header in the section you are in with the previous section. What results is that, in our example of this book, my chapter title "Headers" will turn my previous chapter's header into "Headers" as well. Or my subsequent chapter header. Or both, depending on the sequence of when I did what.

By unchecking Link to Previous, each section will then stand alone. That means you can give each chapter a unique chapter header.

It may take several runs through your manuscript to make sure all breaks and links are proper. But once they are, Microsoft Word will do what you have told it to do and your headers will align perfectly.

Headers

If you need a place to begin learning more about headers, please go to Microsoft.com. You can also search online for your own tutorials about headers.

Headers should provide enough information to help your reader know where in the book he is. Like you have done with pagination, make sure your section breaks and links are properly formatted.

Checklist

☐ The format I choose for my headers is:

_____

☐ I have double checked all **breaks** and **Links to Previous**.

☐ See Microsoft.com for more information about headers.

Chapter 13

Make it Fancy

Some books, heavy on description or facts, work best without any extra visual elements. Others become almost works of art when you liven things up visually. Whether you add visual elements to your manuscript or not and what those visual elements might be, depends on many variables.

The number one variable to consider is your genre. Obviously, a chapter icon of a bouquet of flowers does not go well in a nonfiction book about space shuttle engineering. But it might go perfectly in an inspirational book for women.

In other words, before you add visual details, make sure you know who your readers are. While genre and readers often go together; they do not always. For example, there might be an equal number of men and women interested in space shuttle engineering. There might also be an equal number of men and women interested in a general inspirational book. But very few men will be reading your book about fashion for women in the 1700's. So be aware of exactly who your specific readers are likely to be and gear your artwork to them, in addition to taking your genre into account.

Here are a few ideas that are commonly used in books along with some ideas for how you might use them for your specific book.

Chapter Icons

A chapter icon is a symbol or simple decoration that follows your chapter title and precedes your text. The Wingdings and Wingdings 2 fonts, standard with Microsoft Word, have several nice symbols that make good chapter icons.

I suggest you open your font style box on the Ribbon. Go to Wingdings and Wingdings 2 and see what is available. Type each font into a Word document, row by row, going back through a second time with your **CAPS button** on to get the second set of symbols.

Then print out the listing of Wingdings and Wingdings 2 and keep it for future reference.

Here are several nice ones you might consider.

◻ I have used this font throughout this book as an example for a unique bullet. This is created in Wingdings 2, by typing in the number 2. It might be a great icon to use for a book about business management, document filing, or a book that utilizes checklists, like this one.

◻   Wingdings, letter r could be similarly used as bullet

♦   Wingdings, letter t could also be used as a bullet. Or using three in a row, centered would make a nice chapter icon, section divider, or indicator of new character point of view. Like this:

♦♦♦

⌘   Wingdings, letter z could be centered like this:

⌘   ⌘   ⌘

❖   Wingdings, letter v centered could be:

❖   ❖   ❖

Typing Wingdings 2; letter c ℘, followed by Wingdings 2, letter d ℘, creates this:

℘℘

Similarly, Wingdings 2; h ℘, followed by Wingdings 2, letter g ℘, creates this:

℘℘

Remember that you can also increase the font size: ℘℘

Or keep the size and bold the font: ℘℘

Dividers

You can also use dividers to separate a chapter summary or section in a nonfiction book. Similarly, you might have a divider when you change point of view in a novel. That divider could emphasize the new character's personality or relate to the book's theme. For example:

For a novel set in Ancient Greece:

For an inspirational book for women:

Or:

The above three examples are from Pixabay.com; used with permission. If you find decorative art you like on the Internet, make sure you have permission to use it commercially, or simply purchase a license. Generally, the cost is not significant.

Text Boxes

I like text boxes. I like the way you can use them to summarize a point. I like to use them to challenge my reader to take the next step. I like to use them to pose a question or give a hint at what is coming up next.

Make it Fancy

By now, you know I like text boxes, because I have included one at the end of each chapter. In this book, I use them to summarize a point.

Here's how to insert a text box into your book. Click on the location where you want your text box. Go to **Insert** on the Ribbon. Find **Text Box** and open the dialogue box.

Select the style text box you prefer. I have used **Simple Text Box**. When you click on it, the text box will open in your document. By clicking and dragging at the corners and edges, you can size the text box. You can also center it or left/right justify it or both with the **Paragraph** box on the Ribbon.

Once you have the text box sized appropriately, click on the center of the box and type in what you want it to contain. By highlighting the text, you can also left/right justify or center the text within the box. You can also change the font type or size within the text box.

Additionally, you can fill the text box. If you have full color in your book, use a color of your choosing for either the text itself or the box. If your book will be black and white, you can still shade the text box for effect. Like this:

The text boxes in this book are plain. They are tidy and no-nonsense. But you can also dress them up with color, shading or *fancy fonts*.

More Extravagant

Obviously, you can get as creative with your book's interior as you like. The caution is to make sure the fanciness adds a visual element but does not jar your reader or make her intellectually dizzy. A little can go a long way when it comes to adding art to your pages.

Speaking of things that can be visually wonderful but have the danger of being too much are to place some of your text onto a background with pattern or texture. Sometimes this is done for the first page of a new chapter; or the page holding a new section title. The background should not be too busy and of course, its use is dependent on whether or not it enhances your specific book and would be well received by your specific reader.

Sometimes, a background pattern is used for only a section of a page. For example, the top quarter of the page of a new chapter might have a background texture. Or the background texture might be used as a border for the page as a whole.

An example of a full-page background pattern might be the use of a light grayscale map of a fantasy world for each section of the book to indicate where the following book section will take place.

Here is an example of a page for a book about home renovation. Maybe this page goes at the end of a chapter, to provide a checklist for the reader or space for the reader to jot down notes for his own project. It could also be used as the first page of a novel set in the Old West.

Similarly, you might create a unique way to set off your chapters. I created the following using Photoshop Elements in less than 3

minutes, with the software's standard background and shape tool. The chapter title could go within the grey rectangle or below the graphic on the white section of the page just before the text.

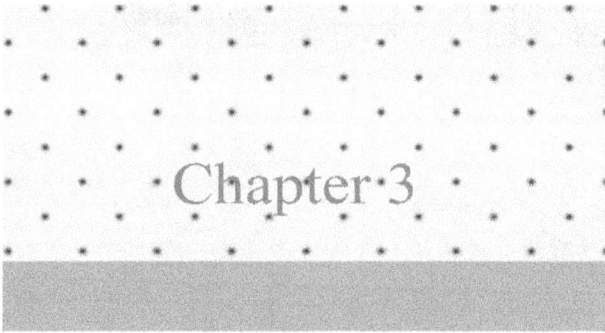

Chapter·3

Full Bleed

Full bleed refers to the printing option that allows images to be printed to the very edge of the paper. The image and therefore the ink, *bleeds* to the edge. Prior to uploading the interior to KDP, it must be sized larger than the ultimate book trim size in order to allow the book to be properly trimmed. It is important therefore to make sure nothing important within the image is close to the page edges that might have to be trimmed away.

If you decide to have artwork as a background or chapter title such as the above two examples, you will also need to select "full bleed" as the printing option when you set up your book. Otherwise, you will have a white border all around your page, which you may not want.

Amazon KDP has excellent instructions about how to handle full bleed in your manuscript. Basically, you must increase the size of your manuscript (see Chapter 3 for how we set the size). That increased size will allow the edges of the manuscript to be trimmed off during printing to ensure that the artwork will extend to the edges without trimming off anything important.

Posh Page Numbers

Page numbers also can be added with flair. Here are some simple examples that can be fun. In order to use something like this, you would *not* use the standard pagination instructions.

Instead, you would need to create a separate graphic for each page. Then turn that graphic into a jpeg file and place it within your document file. Since doing that for a 200-page book would be tedious (and visually taxing to your reader), you might consider creating jpeg page numbers only for the first pages of chapters.

As before, I created these three jpeg page numbers in Photoshop Elements, using their standard graphics and fonts. (Used with permission via licensing.)

Illustrations in Novels

Illustrations in novels are rare. Basically, the delight of novels is from the presentation of the story and characters. But sometimes some sort of illustration could add to the book's interest.

For example, you might include a grayscale map of the solar system in which your space travel book takes place. Similarly, you might include an engineering design of some tech you invented for your characters, or a drawing of their star ship.

If you don't feel artistic, even a listing of vocabulary used by your fantasy world characters or something about your novel's unique location could be an interesting visual element. Vocabulary or information about the location is usually placed directly before the beginning of the book, so the reader has that information handy before starting to read.

Illustrations in Nonfiction

We tend to think of illustrations for adult readers as more naturally occurring in nonfiction. In nonfiction books, sometimes facts, figures, and statistics can be understood more clearly visually. Consider whether your information is best displayed in a graph, chart, line bar, pie chart, list or photograph. In fact, you might need more than one type of graphic to clarify information.

Graphs and charts can be created using a drawing software and put into grayscale. Microsoft Power Point and Microsoft Word have the ability to create simple graphics. Because Power Point and Word are part of the total Microsoft Office suite, it is simple to then input those graphics into your book interior.

Make it Fancy

Remember that utilizing a grayscale instead of full color within your manuscript will lower the cost of production. You can then pass that cost savings on to your buyer or increase the royalty to yourself.

When considering grayscale, you are not limited to just different shades of gray. Instead, you might have some of the information presented using hashes, texture, or patterns.

Photographs are another visual element that can be added to nonfiction work. Images of people in memoirs or biographies or photographs of locations and objects clarify information presented in the written text and bring people and events to life. Make sure, however, that you have permission to use photographs of other people and/or taken by other people.

Make sure also that the photographs are of a quality to add value to the book. Blurred photographs are often better left out if you are unable to have them increased in clarity.

Make it Fancy

Again, keep the cost factor in mind when deciding whether to use black and white or color photos. If you only have one or two color photographs or charts in your book, you must still select the option of white paper/color, which increases the total cost of your book.

> You can be clever with the visual elements. Keep in mind the genre you have written, your reader's taste and expectations, and whether the visual element adds or detracts from their value to your reader.

Checklist

☐ The visual elements that make sense for my book are:

    ☐ Chapter icons

    ☐ Chapter dividers

    ☐ Background patter (and full bleed)

    ☐ Fancy page numbers

    ☐ Illustrations

    ☐ Graphs/charts

    ☐ Photographs

☐ I will use grayscale or color: _____

Chapter 15

Children's Book Illustrations

The topic of children's book interiors needs a set of volumes of its own. Many writers of adult books, however, often find that they have one or two children's books "in them" to write. So, let's give a short preview of illustrated children's books.

Picture Books by Age

Infant to age 2: this includes board books, cloth books, and books about babies, but includes traditional paper-page books as well. An example is *Ten Little Fingers and Ten Little Toes*, by Mem Fox.

Age 2-4: this is the golden age for picture books. They contain simple stories with a beginning, middle, end; with problem and resolution/lesson learned. These books are also typically read-aloud books since the child generally does not yet read. An example is *Little Blue Truck*, by Jane Schertle.

Age 5-7: This age range includes more complex stories. Illustrations may tell a different or opposite story. They often include more humor and more complex problems and are often read-alone books. An example are the *Arthur* books by Marc Brown.

There is an additional, more narrow market for **ages 7-10**. This market includes picture books that may supplement classroom learning. An example would be Greg Tang's *Grapes of Math* picture book (grades 2-5).

Illustrations

Often, an illustrator's interpretation of the text will not just supplement the story. Often the illustrations will take the story into a deeper or entirely new direction. Often an illustrator can tell a unique, opposite, or ironic story with illustrations. Too many written descriptions can therefore hinder the creativity an illustrator brings to the finished picture book.

I suggest you go through your text. Highlight everything that "could" be told through illustrations—facial expressions, colors, actions (such as "he walked to the corner"; "he sat down"), detailed descriptions. Then go back and thoughtfully determine if those are absolutely necessary to the story. If not, hit the "delete" key and move on.

If, of course, you intend illustrations to show something different than what your text says, make sure to add a short illustration note in the text, so an editor, agent or illustrator will "get" what you intend. But use illustration notes sparsely and only where necessary. And of course, if you are independently publishing your book, make sure to delete those illustration notes from the final book when uploaded.

Go through your manuscript and look also at the number of scenes you have created. A picture book is generally 24 pages (sometimes 32; always divisible by 4 because of how they are assembled). You need to make sure there is enough action and scenes to fill the pages of the book.

Illustrations need to show scenes and each one should be different. A book filled with 24 pages of the child looking sad and 1 page looking happy doesn't make for an interesting visual set. Does your story have enough change, scenes, and action to create 12-24 different, exciting, and varied illustrations?

Many picture book writers create "dummies." This is a way of sketching out the story to assure adequate illustration possibilities. It also helps authors look for places for appropriate page turns and where a full spread illustration might occur to slow the pace or provide a transition or where multiple, smaller illustrations grouped on one page could affect pacing, either to speed up or slow down the story.

Although you can find samples of picture book dummies online, a simple thing to do is to just fold 6 sheets of paper into quarters to give you 24 "boxes." Then write out your text, spreading it across the boxes as you see it. Note (or draw) what you envision for illustrations (keeping in mind that they will be up to the editor and illustrator to determine). Do you have large chunks of text on some pages and very little on others? Does that work or would it be better if text were more evenly split? How do the "page turns" land?

Familiarize yourself with how other picture books are created. Note the page turns. Note where the illustrator has developed a full spread over 2 pages or has continued an illustration over a page turn. Look at perspective, color, tone, and detail. Understand what goes into the illustration half of picture book storytelling. If you do, your own half of the telling will be richer because of it.

An excellent example of how an illustrator tells a side story through illustrations is Jan Brett's *The Mitten.*

Non-Picture Books for Children

In addition to picture books broken down by age and category, there are other types of books for children. Most of those, such as middle grade novels, do not include any type of illustration.

Some books, such as easy readers or early chapter books may have a simple illustration at the beginning of a chapter. These books generally transition readers from picture books to middle grade novels as their ability to read improves. The purpose of these simple illustrations is partly to help the child understand the concepts and words in the text by giving them visual clues. They also provide a sense of continuity and comfort as the child moves into this new, more difficult reading. Most of the illustrations therefore in easy readers and early chapter books are simple black and white illustrations.

For you as an author publishing these early readers or early chapter books, it means the cost of production will be less because you can select black and white for your interior. The cost will also be less because your illustrator will be creating fewer, simpler illustrations for you.

◆◆◆

The best advice when thinking about creating a children's book is to head to the bookstore or library. Pull out several dozen books and start studying them. How do the illustrations and text go together? Do they complement each other? Do the illustrations tell a different or opposite story?

Children's Book Illustrations

How are the illustrations laid out on the page? When does the illustrator display several illustrations on a page? When does the book show a full spread on two facing pages? What is the effect of doing that? How do page turns affect the illustrations and the story?

Then start planning your own illustrations. Keep your reader in mind through it all. How can you make a child love your book?

For a picture book you have to create a complete story, character development, problem resolution, conflict, theme, and satisfying ending in under 500 words. Then you must leave half of the story to be told by the illustrator. But when done well, they are part art and part love.

Checklist

☐ The age range for the children's book I am working on is:

_____

☐ I expect it to have _____ illustrations.

☐ The illustrator for this book will be: _____

Chapter 15

Front Matter

When we were ten, we could scratch out a title on construction paper, end our manuscript with *The End* and we were done. Now that we are in the business of producing published books to sell, there is a bit more to the process. In fact, our manuscript is only part of the pages that fill a book. The rest is either front matter or back matter. Although not all pieces of front or back matter are required in every book, most are important, and each has a purpose.

Front matter simply refers to the pages that appear before page one of the book. Back matter refers to the pages that appear in the book after the end.

If we follow industry standards, there are specific requirements for what each page should include and where it should be placed within the book. Remember also that front matter is not included within the pagination of the manuscript. Although the norm in earlier years was to paginate this information using small case Roman numerals, that is no longer common. Therefore, keep it simple and leave your front matter without any kind of pagination.

Let's first discuss the front matter in the traditional order they are placed within the front section of a book.

Full Title Page

The full title page is a must. Yes, you have the book's title right there on the cover. But it is reassuring for the reader to open the book and see it again there right at the front.

The full title page (as opposed to a half title page which we will talk about later) includes:

- The book title

- The subtitle if any

- Author's name

- Publisher

- Series title, if any

That's it. There is plenty of white space on the page. It's neat and clean and says only what is required. Don't try to add anything else. Don't delete anything. Title, subtitle, author's name, publisher, and series.

You will, of course, want to use a fairly large font for this page. Otherwise the information will seem unimportant to the reader. In reality, you want this information to stand out proudly.

You may, as many publishers do, use the same or a similar style font for the book's title on the full title page as the one used on the book cover. You do not, however, need to use the same font style or size for all of the information on the page

A subtitle on this page can be in the same style font or a different one from the title on the title page. It is generally also centered on the page and fairly close in space to the main title.

There follows a larger space on the page and then the author's name is printed. It will often be spaced mid-way on the page and it also is in a fairly large font, although generally smaller than the title.

The publisher's name will be in smaller font and at the bottom center of the page. If you have a publishing entity, you might use the font you typically use for that entity. Additionally, a publishing entity logo fits well on the full title page.

The very first page of this book you are reading, is an example of a full title page.

Copyright Page

The copyright page should be the second page of the book, on the left-hand side. Here is included:

- Publishing year

- Copyright information

- Disclaimer

- Book design information (optional)

- The ISBN is frequently listed

A good idea is to check the copyright page of several published books. See how they set up the page and what order they include what information. Feel free to go to the copyright page of this book and see how I did mine.

On this page I also like to give credit for any graphics, references, or software I use, making sure to address the issue of licensing or permission. In all things, if you are using information, resources, or artwork created by someone else, make sure you have their permission to use it. Make sure also that you have obtained any required licenses and that those licenses are appropriate. In other words, make sure you have a license that allows you to use it for commercial work.

Dedication Page

This page is not essential or required in your book. But it is nice. Here is where you write one sentence or two, dedicating your book to someone who has encouraged your writing or inspired the creation of this book.

Don't turn the dedication into its own chapter. This is an example of when less is more. Make it simple but make it heartfelt.

The Dedication Page is not a necessary part of the front matter. I have included one in this book. You can use it as an example for yours.

Epigraph

This is a fancy word that just refers to a short quote, Scripture, poem, or quote from the book itself. It is a teaser.

As you would expect, the epigraph is not an essential part of a book and is the exception, rather than the rule.

Often authors will begin a chapter or new section with an epigraph to prepare the reader for what is to come. I sometimes use one to present a theme in a novel. For example, in my middle grade novel, *Stealing Sunlight*, the epigraph is:

The day I learned I could fly, was the worst day of my life.

The Epigraph is not a necessary part of the front matter. I have created one for this book in order to show you an example. It is located within the front matter, between the Dedication and the Table of Contents. The Epigraph is typically created without a title.

Table of Contents

Next comes the table of contents; sometimes now just called *Contents.* This will break the book into sections and chapters and will include the page numbers where they can be found.

Some more technical books might include subsections within the table of contents. As with all things, however, remember that the purpose is to assist the reader. You want to clarify the contents of the book; not overwhelm your reader with the wealth of knowledge it contains.

Microsoft Word allows you to create a table of contents with a few mouse clicks. You may also customize your table with a different font style or size than the default. The beauty of the software however, is that once the Table of Contents has been created, it can be changed if you later make changes to your content.

To create a table of contents, click on **References** on the Ribbon. Then click on the down arrow at Table of Contents to open the dialogue box. Select one of the present formats or click on **Custom Table of Contents**.

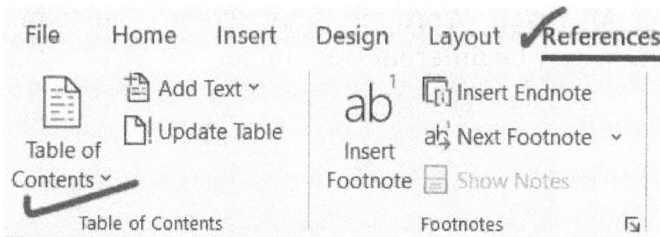

It should then ask you how many levels of heading you want for your book. I typically select just the chapter titles (level one). I therefore need to go to **Options** and delete the levels I do not want.

You will also see that there is an option to create hyperlinks for your book. That will be useful when you turn your book into an E-book. For your print book, unclick the hyperlink option.

If you later add a chapter or a paragraph that changes the pagination, you simply go to the **Ribbon→References→Update Table**. If you have not added a great deal of text, you may simply need to update pages. Otherwise, you may need to update the whole table of contents.

If you create your Table of Contents and find that the Microsoft default font is different from the one you selected for your interior, you can easily change it. Simply select the text of the Table to highlight it. Then Go to the font selection box on the Home tab of the RIBBON. Select the font type and size and enter. It should change the whole Table of Contents to the selected font and size.

One last piece of advice: When you go through your final editing process, make sure to include the table of contents in your editing. Often page numbers move about within the body of the book during revision. Make sure, therefore that the Table of Contents reflects the actual location of chapter beginnings.

See the Table of Contents in this book as an example of how I created a customized table of contents. Remember that your version of Microsoft Word or your screen's customization or configuration may be different from mine.

Front Matter

Acknowledgment(s) Page

The Acknowledgment is generally one or two pages in length. This is different from the Dedication page. Here the author thanks people who have helped get the book written or published. Perhaps someone gave you the idea for the book. Or you had several beta readers give you feedback on an early version. Maybe someone edited your book for you, designed the cover or helped you with the technology of publication.

The Acknowledgment page is where you acknowledge people who have been instrumental in the book creation process.

The Acknowledgment page is not a necessary part of the front matter. I have included an Acknowledgment page here as an example and to thank my friend Mary Vine for her editing help, JoEllen Claypool for writing the Foreword to this book, and my husband for technical advice.

Foreword

The Foreword is generally written by someone other than the author. This person tells the reader about the author, about the book, and how they are connected to the writer of the Foreword.

You might have a Foreword to a book about health, written by a medical doctor or researcher, or a person who worked with you on writing the book, which resulted in benefit to them personally.

Often the Foreword can be used as a marketing tool for the book. It is basically a recommendation of the book, encouraging your readers why the book will be of value to them.

Front Matter

The Foreword is not a required part of the front matter. My writing colleague and professional editor, JoEllen Claypool, wrote the Foreword for this book.

Preface

The Preface is written by the author. The preface talks about the book. The author may share the source of inspiration for the book or the writing process the author went through. Often, the preface helps defend the book, by giving information about how and why the author came to write it.

The Preface is not a necessary part of the front matter, but I have included one in this book as an example.

Introduction

The Introduction tells the reader what they can expect from the book. The introduction explains what is important about the book or its subject matter. It might explain the organization of the book or suggest ways to implement thoughts contained in the book. The introduction shares with the reader what they need to know in order to get the most from the book.

In the Introduction to this book, I included a notice, advising my readers that the book is not an instruction book on how to use Microsoft Word. Rather, the Introduction encourages my readers to use the terms presented to search for instructions or tutorials online to help them with their individual word processing system.

That type of information within the Introduction to a book helps set the reader's expectations so that if the reader's screen does not exactly reflect the screen shots in this book, she will remain calm and seek outside help as it relates to her personal computer configuration or software version.

The Introduction is not a required part of the front matter. I have included one in this book as an example.

Prologue

The Prologue is generally limited to fiction books. It is basically a scene that comes before the story. The prologue helps the reader understand the chronology or the plot to come.

Be aware that some readers hate prologues, preferring to dive right into the story. Your story might need a prologue. Nonetheless, keep in mind that if your specific reader doesn't like them, it won't get read.

The Prologue is not a necessary part of the front matter. Because this book is nonfiction, I did not include a prologue.

Half Title Page

The Half Title Page is what it sounds like. It is half (or actually less than half) of what is contained on the Full Title Page. Basically, the Half Title Page is just the book title—usually in the same font style and size as the Full Title Page.

The Half Title Page, however, does not contain a subtitle. It does not contain the author's name or the publisher. The title is listed mid-way on the page.

The purpose of the Half Title Page is to separate the front matter from the beginning of the book. It visually alerts the reader to what's to come. It says:

Are you ready, reader? Turn the page and start the journey!

The Half Title Page is not a required part of the front matter, but when you understand the purpose behind it—to visually alert the reader to the beginning of the book, it does add a nice touch to your book's interior.

I included a Half Title Page within the front matter of this book as an example. It is located just after the Introduction (since I do not have a Prologue) and just before Chapter 1. Notice that the Half Title Page is itself not titled as such.

What to Include and Why

As you have become familiar with the various elements of what can (and what should) go into the front matter section of your book, you can see that this is an area of your book that you can either expand or shorten, depending on the overall page length of your book and keeping your reader's expectations in mind. It can also increase or reduce the cost of production of your book. So, think through what you want to include or leave out of the front matter. Make sure the inclusion of pages adds value to your book.

In the area of production cost savings, some authors choose to combine the Half Title and the Copyright Page into one. They then follow with the Full Title Page and the remaining front matter they have chosen to include. You only save one page, but one page is something you might want to consider for your book.

Those pages comprise the front matter of books. While you may not include all of those pages in all of your books, you likely will include several. Placing them in the order that is standard publishing industry practice gives your book a look of professionalism and adds credibility to you as an author who knows what goes into books. And you gain that credibility right up front, just as the reader opens the book. It is worth the effort to get it right.

It is time to create your book's front matter.
What will you include?

Checklist

I will include the following pages in the front matter of my book:

- ☐ Full Title Page

- ☐ Copyright

- ☐ Dedication

- ☐ Epigraph

- ☐ Table of Contents

- ☐ Acknowledgement

- ☐ Forward

- ☐ Preface

- ☐ Introduction

Front Matter

- ☐ Prologue
- ☐ Half Title Page

Chapter 16

Back Matter

Just as we saw with the front matter, the back matter of a book can contain several different items. Not all of them are required for each book. Let's look at them one at a time, in the order they should be presented in your book.

Epilogue

For fiction only, an epilogue is a step in the story beyond the story's resolution. It may be an additional scene that takes place later in time or elsewhere at the same time. It might be a view from a different character's point of view. It might be a hint of something to come, indicating, for example, a new book in a series.

One thing about an epilogue, however, is that it must be relevant. It must also contain a wow moment. And, perhaps most importantly, it should not be something that should have been included within the main body of the story.

The Epilogue is not a necessary part of the back matter. I have not included one in this nonfiction book.

Back Matter

Acknowledgments Page

This page can be at the beginning of the book, within the front matter (see Chapter 15). Some authors, however, prefer to place it at the end of the book.

The Acknowledgment would include the same information whether it was located within the front matter or back matter.

The Acknowledgment is not a necessary part of the front matter or the back matter. Because I have included an Acknowledgment Page in the front matter of this book as an example, none is contained in the back matter.

Discussion Section

Novels and self-help or inspirational books are popular with book clubs. Many authors therefore include a section in the back matter with discussion questions. That section encourages book clubs to select the book, increasing sales for the author.

Sometimes the discussion questions are organized by chapter. Sometimes they are organized by character or theme for novels.

A Discussion Section is not a necessary part of the back matter for a book. I have not included a Discussion Section in the back matter of this book. If a group of writers selected this book for a writing book club, I would suggest they use the prompts at the end of each chapter for their discussion.

Appendix or Appendices

An Appendix (singular) is a section within the back matter that contains supplementary information. An example of an Appendix for a nonfiction book about setting up a business, might be a template for creating a business plan. An Appendix for a book on healthy eating might include instructions for dinner planning or a selection of nutritious recipes.

Within the back matter of this book are two Appendices (plural). Appendix A provides my reader with a series of prompts to help develop a book project. Appendix B is a step-by-step guide to creating a file storage system.

The Appendix is not a necessary part of the back matter.

Glossary

The Glossary is a listing of words and terms used in the book. It includes definitions and translations for foreign words. The Glossary lists words and terms alphabetically. It generally does not include page numbers where the words and terms are located. Because foreign words are required to be italicized within documents, they are also italicized within the Glossary.

Glossaries are especially helpful in textbooks, educational books, and nonfiction books for children who may not be familiar with certain words or terms.

The Glossary is not a necessary part of the back matter. I have included a Glossary in the back matter of this book as an example. Microsoft Word has a tool that will create a Glossary for you. It can be found in the Ribbon under the References tab. I did not use the tool when I created the Glossary at the back of this book. It took me approximately one hour to create the Glossary without the tool, just by going through the manuscript, looking for important terms and then copying and pasting them into a Glossary and adding their definition.

Bibliography or Sources

Bibliography is the traditional term used for the listing of resources used in the research and preparation of the book. The more modern term used is Sources, but both names serve the same purpose.

This page of the back matter gives the author credibility. It supports the author's position or claims set out in the book. It is therefore highly recommended for most nonfiction books. It is rare as part of fiction back matter, but occasionally an author might create one for example, for research done on a book of historical fiction.

A Sources page is included within the back matter of this book for your reference. I have used the *MLA Style Manual* for my guide in this book's preparation and have therefore listed it on my Sources page. The APA (Associated Press) and Chicago style guides are other often-used guides, along with many others available to writers. They include rules for punctuation and citing sources as well as other aspects of writing for publication. Strictly follow the style guide you use when listing sources. Make sure you are consistent throughout.

A Bibliography or Sources page is not a necessary part of the back matter. It is, however, recommended for nonfiction books that contain facts and statistics the reader might want to verify.

Index

The Index is a list of terms used in the book with accompanying page numbers where those topics can be found. The difference between an index and a glossary is that the Glossary includes definitions and no page numbers. A glossary is basically a dictionary.

The Index on the other hand, is more like a search engine. It lists terms and topics covered in the book and indicates where they can be found.

Both a glossary and index are often included in children's nonfiction books. Their inclusion within the back matter affects their salability within the children's educational market.

The Index is not a necessary part of the back matter. I have included an Index in the back of this book as an example. Microsoft Word includes a tool to create an Index. I did use the tool to create my Index. It is found on the Ribbon under the References Tab→Index. It took approximately 30 minutes to create the 2-column Index for this book using the Microsoft tool.

Colophon

The Colophon includes additional publisher and design information. This information may be included in the front matter after the title page. Sometimes it is included on the Copyright Page, as I have done in this book.

The Colophon is not a necessary part of the back matter. I have not included one in this book because that information is presented on the Copyright Page.

Author's Thanks

Although this page might traditionally be placed later within the back matter, it makes sense for most authors to move it up to shortly after the end of the manuscript.

As an author, we want to tell our readers how much we appreciate them buying and reading our book.

We also want to ask them to recommend our book to others right now, while the book is fresh in their minds.

Included in the Author's Thanks could be an invitation for the reader to review the book on Amazon.com. Simple instructions for how they would find the book on Amazon and what buttons to click to leave a review are helpful and appreciated by the reader who may feel technically inhibited.

A short author bio can be left on this page also, along with a citation of where the reader can find the author online. Or a separate author bio can be placed later in the back matter.

Author's Thanks is not a necessary part of the back matter, however, thanking your reader is something we should do. I have included an Author's Thanks page in the back matter of this book as an example.

Books by Author

Although this list will change as you write more books, it is a good plan to include this list in every book you write. You might even list one or two books you are in the process of writing, if you are sure you will be publishing them soon. In those cases, you could list your books as:

Books available or coming soon:

On this page list your online presence again. Make it easy for people to connect with you and become your fans!

The Books by Author page is not a necessary part of the back matter. I have included one as an example. You can organize your books alphabetically, by genre, or date published, or as I have done, by publisher.

Other Back Matter Goodies

When it comes to front matter, good advice is to generally follow the rules. Include what is traditionally included in front matter, if it makes sense to you and your specific book. And follow the traditional order for those pages.

When it comes to the main body of your book, follow traditional advice, adding visual elements when they make sense, if they do not visually overwhelm your reader.

When it comes to back matter, you have a bit more leeway. You have already proven to your reader that you know the rules and can follow them. Hopefully, by the time your reader gets to the back matter, he is already on your side. Your reader is anxious to see what other goodies you have included, now that he has completed your wonderful book.

When it comes to back matter then, think about what might be helpful or interesting to your readers.

Author Bio or About the Author: If you have not included an author bio on your Author's Thanks page, you might do one. Often the Author Bio might be located on the book's back cover or jacket flap, if you have one. An Author Bio can help give the author credibility or likability. You might include a professional head shot here—one that reflects the writing brand you are creating. I have included an About the Author page within my back matter, placed directly after my Books by Author page.

Additional Verses: In my book *The Praying Writer,* I include verses of Scripture in each chapter. Within the back matter, then, I also add additional verses related to various aspects of writing.

Educational Supplement: In my children's books, if appropriate, I add information at the back of the book that has an educational element to it. For example, my middle grade novel *Hydro Phobia*, takes place partly in Mexico and partly at Niagara Falls. I have also made up a technology, based in part on real science. At the end of the book, therefore, I have information about the locations in the book and explain the real science upon which I base my invented technology.

Similarly, you might indicate what specific curriculum (or Common Core) standards or subject matter, age, and grade level your book could relate to.

Other Extras: At the end of your how-to book, you might include checklists or suggestions and instructions for how your reader might utilize the information in your book.

Or if your novel is set in the Old South, you might include a recipe for one of the food items your main character loved.

Consider what you could include at the end of your book to enhance your book's content and give added value to your reader.

◆◆◆

Back Matter

Have fun with the extras you might include in your back matter. If they work in your book, fantastic. If they are a fabulous idea but don't necessarily feel right within your particular book, add a link to your website and provide those recipes, location photographs, or additional book elements online. Even if they are not part of your book, they may still be a way to engage your reader beyond the covers of your book.

> Back matter can provide extra value to your reader,
> beyond what is contained in the main body of your book.
> Explore how you can help or delight your reader with
> additional information. Give your reader more than she
> expected and entice her to see what your next book will bring.

Checklist

I want to include the following pages in the back matter of my book:

- ☐ Epilogue

- ☐ Acknowledgments Page

- ☐ Discussion Section

- ☐ Appendix

- ☐ Glossary

- ☐ Bibliography or Sources

Back Matter

- ☐ Index

- ☐ Colophon

- ☐ Author's Thanks

- ☐ Other Books by Author

- ☐ Other Goodies

Chapter 17

A Few More Techie Things

Embedding Fonts

Embedding fonts is a process which ensures that all the font information used to make your document look the way it does is stored in the PDF file. This is important when a PDF file is transmitted to a different computer system (such as Amazon's KDP). That computer system might use a different reading software than yours. That means the computer reader at that end may automatically render fonts differently from what you intended.

Problems might also occur if a font you have used does not allow for a commercial application at KDP's end of the screen. For example, if you purchased a particularly unique font for your book, KDP may not have the licensing right to use that font for publication. You, however, having purchased the licensing right, *can* use it. Embedded fonts within your file may therefore lessen KDP's liability.

The process of embedding fonts will not affect the look of your book. In fact, it helps assure that the look of your book is consistent with the PDF you originally transmitted. Therefore, KDP requires that your book interior fonts be embedded. The good news is that Amazon KDP will embed them for you.

There's great satisfaction, however, on those sometimes rare occasions when you launch the book previewer and it starts out with: We found no errors.

As independent publishers, we are trying to be professional. We are trying to do things as they are done in the publishing industry. We therefore, might as well know how to embed fonts in our manuscripts ourselves.

These are KDP's instructions on is how to embed your fonts in your book interior prior to uploading to KDP. Remember that your screen configuration may appear slightly different from these screen shots.

- Go to the **File** tab and select **Options** at the very bottom of the left-hand column.

- Under the "Save" tab of that new dialogue box, check the **Embed fonts in the file** box.

- Make sure the **Embed only the characters used in the document** and **Do not embed common system fonts** boxes are both unchecked.

- Click OK.

- Then, return to the **File** tab on the Ribbon. Select **Save as**. Choose where to save the file on your computer. In the "**Save as type**" dropdown menu, select **PDF** and click Save.

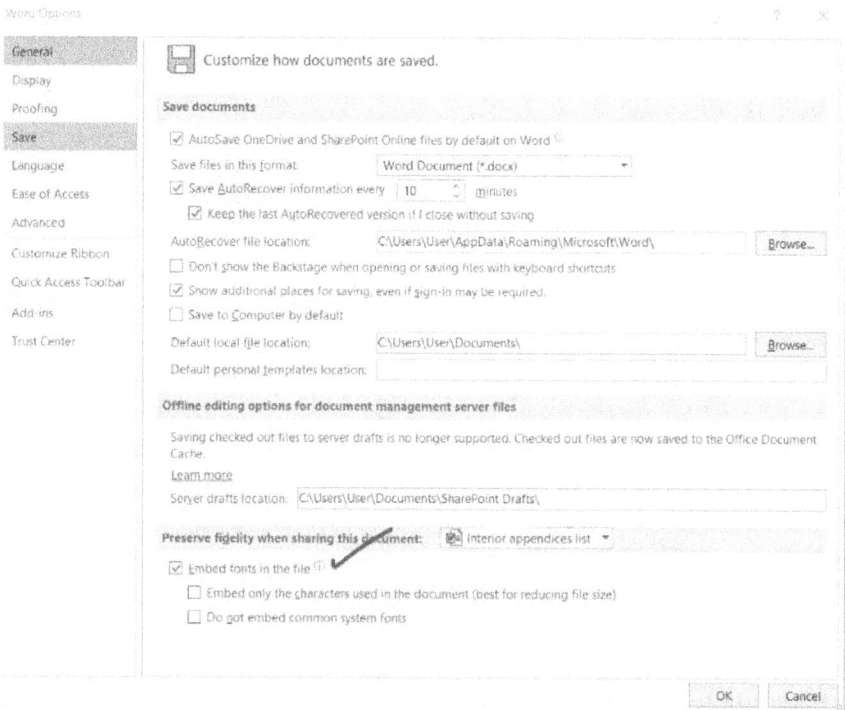

Your file is now saved as a PDF with embedded fonts, ready to upload to KDP.

Keep a Critical Eye on Graphics

Make sure you have created crisp and clean graphics. Illustrations, such as charts and graphs are there to help clarify information. A fuzzy illustration doesn't clarify; nor does it give your reader confidence of the accuracy of the information presented. Make sure your graphics look professional and they will be received with more trust.

If you are including photographs or decorative items, make sure you use an adequately high **dpi (dots per inch)** when creating them. Things that look fine on a computer screen may not look as good when printed. This is especially true if your interior is printed on cream paper. Cream paper is generally more porous; therefore lines may be slightly distorted at the fine level.

E-Book Formatting

As a general rule, if you are creating an electric version of your book for upload to Amazon KDP, your PDF format is usually adequate. You will first, of course, want to change your Table of Contents to remove page numbers and instead have hyperlinks. Then when your reader taps on a chapter title, she will automatically be taken to that part of the electronic book, without having to scroll through it by hand.

Once you upload the file for the electronic book, then make sure to view it in the various simulated devices, to see that all formatting looks appropriate. If you have a great deal of special formatting—such as for the examples in this book—your standard PDF file may not display perfectly in all of the simulated devices. If that happens, you may need to consider reformatting your file into MOBI format and re-uploading it.

MOBI is a format that is created specifically for low bandwidth mobile devices. There are several free forms of software that can convert your PDF files into MOBI files. Or you will likely be able to find someone who will convert your file for a relatively low cost.

A Few More Techie Things

Saving Files

Saving files goes without saying. Because it is important. Therefore, let's go ahead and say it.

Save your files in a way you can easily know which file is most current. There are many types of file systems people use. Some people date their files, so they recognize which is the most current version. Other people use different word cues to keep things organized.

Appendix B at the back of this book is a step-by-step guide to one of many possible file savings systems you might use for your book project(s). Coincidently, it is the system I use.

Backing Up Your Work

Saving files is about having a system to be able to locate individual projects you are working on. Backing up your work is about keeping that work safe from loss.

The secret to backing up your work is to do so often—daily, weekly, or at least monthly. My rule is that any time I have spent more than 2 hours on my work, I back it up.

Also part of backing up your work is to do so in multiple places. Keep your file on your desktop. Copy it to your C drive, D drive, and X, Y, and Z drives. Save it on an external hard drive and a USB drive. Save it on a floppy disk if you still have one.

Then save it in the cloud. Email it to yourself. Send it to your writing friend.

A Few More Techie Things

We have all lost work. We have lost files. We have thought we had saved things only to not find where they went. Or not have the latest version.

It sounds silly to save the same thing multiple times in multiple places. It's better to sound silly and still have your work though, than think you've saved that final, copyedited book and find later you have to start over from the last time you backed it up—75 hours of work later.

◆◆◆

There is more to publishing books than just writing a story or typing a manuscript. Part of the process is creative; part is technical. Much of it involves a steep learning curve. But each part is important, and each part deserves your best effort to make your book the best it can be.

> There is a lot to learn and a lot to remember in independent book publishing. One of the most important things to remember is to save your work and back it up often. Do you?

Checklist

☐ Do you embed your fonts? Do you need additional help in learning how? See the Sources page at the back of this book for where to go for further information.

A Few More Techie Things

- ☐ Do you have graphics in your book? Are they clear and easily understandable? Do you need to redo any of them for publication?

- ☐ Do you need to format your E-book file into a MOBI file?

- ☐ Do you have a consistent system for saving files so you can easily find the most current one?

- ☐ Do you have a consistent system for backing up files? If you have not done so, calendar your file backup for no less than monthly and plan to at least email your latest work to yourself at the end of your workday.

Chapter 18

Putting It Together

We can create a fantastic novel. We can write a helpful how-to. We can explain the hard to explain. That writing, however is only part of what goes into creating a book.

A book is a product. Whether the book is printed on paper or viewed on electronic screens, it is something our readers hold in their hands. It is also visual. How our book looks visually can enhance or detract from the words it contains.

As an author, you may think you are only interested in creating memorable characters or intriguing stories set in unusual locations. As a writer, you may focus solely on informing your readers of important concepts in your world.

But publishing a book without thinking about visual elements that complement the words, story, or topic, is doing an injustice to your reader and doing nothing to raise your standard of professionalism.

What if, instead, you became known as the author whose books are not only valuable to read, but pleasurable to read because they are presented in a visually attractive way?

What if at a subconscious level, your reader senses that the layout structure of your book helps them assimilate information more easily?

Wouldn't you like to read books which do that?

So do your readers.

There is a lot of information in this book. Some of it may not feel appropriate for the books you presently write or for the writing brand you are trying to develop. In fact, the purpose of this book is *not* to encourage you to use all visual elements listed here. You may use one element or three or none. The key is to make your book experience pleasant for your reader. You want to clarify, enhance, and encourage your reader—never to overload your reader visually.

Hopefully, there are some things presented here that strike you as right for you. Take those suggestions and make them your own.

Best wishes in your writing journey!

Carol Peterson

Appendix A

Think About Your Book

This form is created to provide you with prompts to help you clarify your thoughts and expand your initial idea for your book.

THE BASICS

Title:_____

This may change over time as your book develops. But give it a title now and the book will feel more real.

If your book is **nonfiction**, what is the Subtitle?

_____

Alternate Subtitle:_____

GENRE

What is the genre of your fiction book? If you feel your book might encompass more than one genre, please mark them in order 1, 2, 3 from the following:

- ☐ Women's Contemporary Fiction
- ☐ Women's Historical Fiction
- ☐ General Contemporary Fiction
- ☐ General Historical Fiction

- ☐ Humor
- ☐ Science Fiction
- ☐ Space Science Fiction
- ☐ Space Opera
- ☐ Cyberpunk
- ☐ Steam punk
- ☐ Dystopian
- ☐ Western
- ☐ Mystery
- ☐ Crime
- ☐ Suspense
- ☐ Horror
- ☐ Contemporary Fantasy
- ☐ High Fantasy
- ☐ Action/Adventure
- ☐ Thrillers
- ☐ Military
- ☐ Alternate History
- ☐ Apocalyptic
- ☐ Children and Young Adult (age: _____)
- ☐ Other: _____

What is the genre of your non-fiction book? Be specific. If you feel your book might encompass more than one genre, please mark them in order 1, 2, 3 from the following:

- ☐ Memoir (your life). What is the focus:

    ___ to record your life in general (chronologically)

    ___ to teach a lesson learned

    ___ to explore a theme

☐ Biography of someone else. What is the focus:

___ to record a life chronologically

___ to teach a lesson learned

___ to explore a theme

☐ Historical event (what is it? _____

What three things about this event are worthy of a book?

_____

_____

_____

How has this historical event impacted you personally?

_____

_____

☐ Exploration of a subject matter (such as a culture, location, medical condition, scientific problem, political issue, philosophical issue, theology, other specific subject matter)

What is it: _____

What is your expertise or experience in the matter that allows you to write about it with authority? _____

_____

_____

☐ To teach a lesson: _____

☐ Is this lesson from study, personal experience, passed on from another or other? _____

☐ To teach a skill or craft (for example, how to knit, how to build a house, crafts for kids, cooking without carbohydrates, exercise, etc.) _____

_____

What is your experience that allows you to write about this with authority? _____

_____

☐ To motivate someone or spur them to action. What do you want the reader to be motivated to do?

_____

_____

☐ Inspirational: What type?
___ faith
___ to accomplish something big
___ other _____

☐ Bible study

Will this cover a specific book of the Bible or be topical?

_____

Do you intend this to be for individual study, group study, church wide study? _____

What Bible version do you intend to use?

_____

Why do you feel you are exactly the right person to write this study? Note any special education or experience you have in Bible study, leading Bible study or other:

_____

After completing this study, what do you expect your reader to have understood better? _____

_____

☐ To persuade someone to your way of thinking. What do you want your reader to conclude after reading your book:

_____
_____
_____

Will this book be highly controversial? Yes/no

Who do you think will be most likely to agree with you up front (demographics: men/women, ages, background, political affiliation, religious affiliation, income bracket)?

_____

_____

Who do you think will be hardest for you to convince about your point of view (demographics: men/women, ages, background, political affiliation, religious affiliation, income bracket)? _____

_____

☐ Collection of poetry. If so, do one of the above additional genres apply (inspirational, motivational, lesson learned, for example)? Which one: _____

☐ Is this book for children?

Age:_____

Genre: _____

YOUR READER

Who specifically are you writing for?

Men or women? _____ Age range: _____

Where do they live? _____

Do they have a specific cultural background, religious affiliation, political affiliation, income bracket?_____

_____

Are you writing this book for a group of people with a specific skill set? For example, teachers, students, mothers, fathers, wives, husbands, leaders, a specific vocational group? What is it?

_____

BOOK PHYSICAL STRUCTURE

- How will this book be offered?

  ☐ E-book

  ☐ print book

- What trim size for a printed book? _____

- Estimated number of pages: _____

- Do you expect this book to be illustrated, for example, with graphs, charts, photographs, tables or other artwork?
  How many illustrations do you envision? _____

  Do those need to be color or black and white? _____

- Do you expect this book to be the first in a series? Yes/no

Will the series be a continuation of this book? Will it be something similar. Examples: fictional episodic; fictional overriding story; Bible study by book or topic; teacher resources by curriculum; recipe books by meal or ingredients.

Appendix B

Creating a File Storage System

Here is one way to create a file storage system for your writing so your projects and most current versions are easy to find.

Create a file folder entitled WRITING

To create a new file on your desktop, first right click anywhere on the screen. A box will show up. Select **New** and follow the arrow **>** to the right to open a second dialogue box. Click on the icon of the file folder which looks like this: 🗁 except it will be vertical and manilla folder colored.

That will create a new (empty) file folder on your desktop. Right click on the new folder and a dialogue box will open. Select **Rename.** The name New folder is now highlighted. Simply type in your new name. I suggest WRITING.

You might instead locate that new file folder on one of your computer drives or even an external drive. When you begin a new writing project, you can then save those projects inside that WRITING folder.

What to Put Inside the Folders

Create a new folder, using the same steps, for each of your major writing projects. For example, if you maintain an online presence, keep a folder named something like ONLINE PRESENCE. In it keep separate documents for your blog posts, content you place on pages of your website, or images you have used or will use. Over time, you might divide those posts by year, creating a separate file folder for each year—within your ONLINE PRESENCE file folder, which is itself nested within your WRITING file folder.

Similarly, when you set out to write a book, organize your work to find it easily. For example, open a new file folder with the title of the book. (Remember you can change the file folder name if you later change the book title.)

Inside that folder, keep separate documents for your storyboarding, your synopsis, your character development, your thoughts about theme, setting, and subplots. Or for your nonfiction book, keep separate documents in that folder for your outline, research, and graphics you create.

Of course, your manuscript document will go in that project folder also.

Naming Your Manuscript Document

Instead of maintaining one long, continuously changing version of your book manuscript, however, I suggest you save the manuscript using a slightly different name for each new revision. Sometimes (not infrequently), you may delete a scene or a topic from your book, only to find later that it fit elsewhere, or you find a way to make it work. If you have deleted that portion of your book, you have to rewrite it. If you rename your new version, however, that work will still be there in an earlier manuscript version—either for the book you are writing or for a future project.

I created a storage filing system for this book. I first gave the project a shortened name so I could find it easily. The shortened name for the project *Inside the Covers* became simply, INSIDE. Then I saved the various manuscript documents by naming them:

INSIDE First Draft

INSIDE Revision 1

INSIDE Revision 2

INSIDE Formatted

INSIDE with front and back matter

INSIDE to upload

Additionally, my INSIDE project file contained a file with documents about research I had done, helpful sources I used, graphics I created, a separate and changing outline, and thoughts about marketing the book.

Some authors use a numbering system for their file storage. So, for example, I could have named my files:

INSIDE 1

INSIDE 2

INSIDE 3

Etc.

Other authors date their files. So for example, I could have saved my files as:

INSIDE 8-12-19

INSIDE 1-14-20

INSIDE 4-28-20

Etc.

Clean Up for Clarity

To tidy up your file folder, at some point you might want to create a new folder within your **project folder**, named Archived or Not Used. I named my file INSIDE Archived.

It is tempting to delete things you don't think you'll ever use. But Word documents take up little computer storage space. I suggest then that you keep everything until (and maybe after) your book is complete, published, and you are sure you won't be doing any major revision.

Instead of wearing out your delete button then, you can place all your previous versions of your manuscript in the archive file. Creating an archive file folder means that when you open up your main project file to work on it, the most recent and most relevant documents will be there to see immediately.

The other benefit of archiving your files is that you are less likely to accidently start working on the wrong document version.

On that happy day when you hold your wonderful book in your hands, you might then create a brand-new file folder. Label it with the short book title and AS PUBLISHED.

INSIDE AS PUBLISHED

In the AS PUBLISHED file will go the final Word document of the manuscript, the manuscript saved as a PDF, the cover file of your book, and Kindle versions of the same. Within that AS PUBLISHED file folder you can also lump everything else into your project archive file, and keep it all safe, making room on your desktop for the next wonderful book project you will create.

Glossary

Acknowledgment or Acknowledgments Page. Part of the front matter where the author thanks people who have helped get the book written or published.

Amazon Kindle Direct Publishing (KDP). Print on demand and e-book publication for authors to independently publish their work.

Appendix (Appendices plural). Part of the back matter that contains supplementary information.

Author Bio. Part of the back matter; short biography about the author's writing experience.

Author's Thanks. Part of the back matter where authors tell their readers how much we appreciate them buying and reading the book.

back matter. The pages that appear in the book after the end.

barcode. The graphical representations of a book's ISBN and price. Barcodes are used on physical books, allowing them to be machine read, and facilitating automated sales and inventory.

Bibliography or Sources. Part of the back matter; a listing of resources used in the research and preparation of the book.

breaks. A command in Microsoft Word that tells the software where you want your text to break and where you want it to begin again on subsequent pages.

> **page break** breaks the text at the end of a page and continues the text on the next page.

section break tells the software to break the document into sections. Section breaks instruct the software about things such as pagination and header/footer placement and content.

chapter icon. A symbol or simple decoration that follows your chapter title and precedes your text.

Colophon. Part of the back matter and includes additional publisher and design information.

cover material. The physical finish for your book's cover.

copyright. The exclusive legal right to reproduce, publish, sell, or distribute the matter and form of something (such as a literary, musical, or artistic work).

Copyright Page. Part of the front matter. It includes publishing year, copyright information, disclaimer, and possibly book design information, ISBN.

copyright registration. Legal process that registers your work publicly as being copyrighted.

Dedication. One or two sentences, dedicating your book to someone who has encouraged your writing or the creation of this book.

Discussion Section. Part of the back matter which provides readers with questions for book clubs.

dropped capital. Increased size of the first letter in the first word of the first paragraph of each chapter, dropping it below the line of text.

embedding fonts. A process which ensures that all font information used to make your document look the way it does is properly stored in the PDF file.

Epigraph. A short quote, Scripture, poem, or quote from the book itself. It may be placed as part of the front matter or a unique epigraph may be placed at the beginning of each chapter.

Epilogue. In fiction; part of the back matter; is a step in the story beyond the story's resolution.

First Page Different. This Microsoft Word instruction allows an author to not include a page number or header on the odd-numbered beginnings of new chapters.

front matter. Refers to the pages that appear in the book before page one of the book.

Foreword. Part of the front matter; is generally written by someone other than the author. This person tells the reader about the author and about the book and how they are connected to them.

full bleed. Refers to the printing option that allows images to be printed to the very edge of the paper.

Full Title Page. The first page of a book; part of the front matter. It includes the book title, a subtitle (if any), author's name, and publisher.

Glossary. A listing of words and terms used in the book.

gutter. The inside margin of the book which allows for adequate space in the seam (center of the book) to read the text.

Half Title Page. Part of the front matter which lists only the title mid-way on the page. The purpose of the half title page is to separate the front matter from the beginning of the book.

headers. Lines of information at the top of each page in books.

Index. A part of the back matter; a list of terms used in the book with accompanying page numbers where those topics can be found.

Introduction. Part of the front matter. It tells the reader what they can expect from the book.

ISBN. Refers to the book's international standard book number assigned to every book before publication. It records details such as the book's language, location of publication, and publisher.

Link to previous. Microsoft Word instruction that links the present section of your document to the previous one.

margins. The white space between the manuscript (text) and the outside edges.

Microsoft Style Guide. Default style guide as part of Microsoft Word, quite dissimilar to standard style guides for writing and publishing.

mirror pages. This setting in Microsoft Word will assure that the margins on both the left side of the page and the right side of the page are identical.

MLA Style Manual. From the Modern Language Association of America. One of several manuals or guides that help publishers maintain consistency throughout their book regarding formatting, grammar, punctuation, and citations.

Other Books by Author. Part of back matter listing other work by the author

Pagination. The process of placing page numbers on a document.

point (abbreviated pt). The size of the font. It refers to the height of the font. Therefore, fonts of different types but the same pt size may appear larger due to the difference in width.

point of view (POV). The story written from one of the character's points of view. We "view" the story through his eyes.

Preface. Part of the front matter written by the author which talks about the creation of the book.

Prologue. Part of the front matter, is generally limited to fiction books. It is basically a scene that comes before the story.

Ribbon. In Microsoft Word, the horizontal section above the white space where you type. The Ribbon contains clickable instructions to help you customize your manuscript.

sans serif. French for *without serif.* A *sans serif* font is one without little tags on the characters.

Serif. French for little tags on the ends of upright parts of characters.

Styles. Tool in Microsoft Word that allows you to preset preferences for font type and sizing, paragraph spacing, indentation and other aspects for your manuscript preparation.

Table of Contents or Contents. Part of the front matter that breaks the book into sections and chapters with the page numbers where they can be found.

text box. A box created in Microsoft Word into which you can type to set off text for visual emphasis.

trim size. A publishing term that refers to the final size your book will be "trimmed" to after printing

white space. The amount of space on the page where text does not appear.

Wingdings: a specialized font that creates decorative symbols when standard letters or numbers on the keyboard are typed.

Sources

Gibaldi, Joseph, *MLA Style Manual*, 2nd ed. New York: The Modern Language Association of America, 1998.

> This is the style manual I prefer. It is commonly used for writing in the humanities (as opposed to technical or scientific writing).

Type Into Print, 3rd ed. New Jersey: Prentice Hall, 1974.

> This is a tried and true book giving lots of information about publishing standards with exhaustive examples.

www.copyright.gov

> This is the official US Copyright Office website. Go here for information about and forms to officially register your work for a copyright.

www.kdp.amazon.com

> This is the website authors can use to independently publish their books with print on demand or Kindle books. KDP has helpful guides and tutorials on how to format your manuscript and book cover and includes templates you canuse that will upload easily to their publishing software.

www.merriam-webster.com

> This website was handy for defining words and terms used in this book.

www.myidentifiers.com

> This is the Bowker Identifier website. There you can purchase ISBNs and barcodes and keep track of the books you have written.

www.microsoft.com

> This site is invaluable for questions about Microsoft Word tools and how to use them.

Index

Author's Thanks

Thank you for reading this book. I hope you read something that will help you with your writing for publication. If this book was valuable to you as a writer, please consider going to Amazon.com and leaving a short review.

Please visit me at my website: CarolPetersonAuthor.com.

Posting an Amazon Review

Locate the book on Amazon.com. Click on the book title to bring up a new page. Or provide the Amazon URL to take your reader directly to your book page.

Scroll to the bottom of the page to Customer Reviews.

Click the "Write a customer review" button.

Click on the number of stars you would give the book.

Amazon should then ask you how you want to post. If you have posted reviews before, it will suggest the name you used previously. If you have never reviewed books, it will lead you to a screen to create your Amazon reviewer identity. Otherwise first name and last initials work fine, or you can create something clever, like Book Addict or Reading Papa. The review name you create is linked to your Amazon account. So next time you post a review, it will remember you.

If you are an author writing a review for another author, you will want to use your own name so that your name is seen in the book world as much as possible.

Click in the *write review box* and type in your review. The review need not be lengthy or inspiring. It's more important to be honest and encouraging to people who might be looking for just what the book offers.

Enter a title for your review. It could be something as simple as "Great book" or "This book helped me..." Sometimes it's easiest to write a review and then enter a title based on a phrase or key word in your review.

After you've finished your review, click *Preview your review*. The screen will show what your review looks like. If it is OK, click *Publish review*. If you want to make changes, click the white *edit* button, make your changes, review it again and then hit *publish review*.

You will receive notice in the email account linked to your Amazon account when your review goes live.

◆◆◆

Note to my reader: Please feel free to copy these review instructions and place them in the back matter of your own books. We writers are a community who love to encourage each other. Please accept this little gift of wording from me to you with my permission.

Books by Author

From Honor Bound Books

Writer's Bookshelf Series. Books available or coming soon:

- *The Write Brand: Becoming Known in the World*

- *The Praying Writer: Prayers for the Writing Process*

- *The Art of the Edit: Developmental, Sequential and Copy Editing*

- *Working Together; Achieving Success: Critiquing, Joint Marketing, Masterminds*

- *Inside the Cover: Fonts, Formatting & Final Touches*

- *Kids' Lit: The Hardest Books You Love to Write*

With Faith Like Hers Bible Study Series: Studies on the character and circumstances of women in Scripture. Books available or coming soon:

- *I am Eve*
- *I am Esther*
- *I am Ruth*
- *I am Mary*
- *I am Elizabeth*
- *I am Rahab*
- *I am Hannah*
- *I am Deborah*

Other books about faith:

- *Flowers, Gemstones & Jesus: Finding Jesus in the Months of the Year*

- *Flowers, Gemstones & Jesus: Special Dates Calendar*

- *Rebuild Your Tattered Temple: Small Beginnings Toward Better Health*

From Mustard Seed Books (an imprint of Honor Bound Books) for children:

- *Counting Blessings* (Picture Book)
- *You, Me & The Sea* (Picture Book)
- *Baby's Day* (Picture Book)
- *Stealing Sunlight* (Middle Grade Novel)
- *Hydro Phobia* (Middle Grade Novel)
- *Seeds of Faith* (the Noah story; Early Chapter Book)

From Libraries Unlimited
Books for teachers to use in classrooms (grades 4-7)

- *Fun with Finance: Math + Literacy = $uccess*
- *Jump into Science: Themed Science Fairs*
- *Around the World Through Holidays: Cross-Curricular Readers Theatre*
- *Jump Back in Time: A Living History Resource*

About the Author

Carol Peterson writes to help writers learn the craft of stringing words together and writes books for children to help them understand this awesome and beautiful world. She also writes books to share God's love with the world through a study of Scripture and opening other's eyes to see evidence of Jesus in the world around them.

Carol is one of four executive directors of Idaho Creative Author's Network (ICAN). ICAN creates workshops and conferences for writers and helps them with writing, editing, publishing, marketing, and networking. You can learn more about ICAN at IdahoCreativeAuthorsNetwork.com.

You can find Carol Peterson online at her website CarolPetersonAuthor.com.

www.ingramcontent.com/pod-product-compliance
Lightning Source LLC
Chambersburg PA
CBHW061721020426
42331CB00006B/1034